THE DISCIPLER
—STUDENT WORKBOOK—

PASTOR PAUL LEACOCK

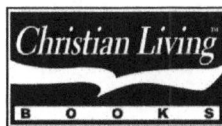

Christian Living
B O O K S

Largo, Maryland
USA

Christian Living Books, Inc.
P. O. Box 7584
Largo, MD 20792
christianlivingbooks.com
We bring your dreams to fruition.

ISBN 9781562293765

CONTENTS

DELINEATING DISCIPLESHIP

DEVELOPING DISCIPLES

Finally, brethren, whatever things are true, whatever things are noble, whatever things are just, whatever things are pure, whatever things are lovely, whatever things are of good report, if there is any virtue and if there is anything praiseworthy - meditate on these things.

(Philippians 4:8)

INTRODUCTION
DEFINING DISCIPLESHIP

Congratulations on your desire to become a disciple of Jesus Christ. You have begun a journey of faith and discipline. These studies have been developed to assist you in making your discipleship journey successful. Every lesson from the beginning to the end is designed to equip you for this wonderful but challenging new way of life.

To begin your journey, you will be introduced to the basic beliefs or tenets of the Christian faith that God the Father wants you to know. This knowledge is crucial and will prove invaluable every step you take. If you are to become a faithful disciple of His Son, the Lord Jesus Christ, you will need to know these fundamental truths of His Word. God's Word is supremely above all other teachings, which may have influenced and shaped your life thus far.

Training in God's truth and all the other aspects involved in this discipleship journey will not be easy. Therefore, if you are to succeed, even to do so with distinction, you will have to be very committed. This means, beginning from now, you will have to adjust your thinking in preparation for serious study and application of the truths you will learn as all true disciples must.

Discipleship training requires your constant and complete devotion. It is a new way of living; therefore, your conscious, deliberate, and determined decision to devote your entire life daily will be necessary. In other words, this training must become your life's top priority.

If you apply yourself diligently, you will profit immensely. Once you take the process of discipleship contained in these lessons seriously, you will see wonderful changes in your personal life. Your new lifestyle will become evident in your relationships, home, work, church fellowship, community, and eventually, in the national and international affairs in which you are involved.

As you live as a disciple, the inspiring, insightful teachings and instructive truths you will be learning are guaranteed to transform you in wonderful ways for the rest of your life. Your discipleship extends beyond this study. Therefore, even when you become a mature disciple, you will look back on this training with a deep sense of gratitude for the great truths learned in your lifetime.

The Lord Jesus Christ wants disciples who commence and complete the journey. The challenges will be demanding; the learning is constant and the opposition will be great.

However, His Spirit will always be with you as you take this journey. To all who would follow Him Jesus said, "If you abide in My word, you are my disciples indeed" (John 8:31).

Thankfully, you don't have to travel alone. You will encounter a series of carefully designed exercises for group interaction to facilitate and encourage you on the discipleship journey. This feature will enhance your learning retention experience as well as enrich your life experience while learning from others.

If you feel the need to venture to a higher level of academic studies, provision is made to facilitate such. For example, each Unit of study ends with opportunities for reflection on the teaching, to "Journalize Your Journey", and to study deeper using the "For Further Study" section.

These sections will prove to be blessings in your life as expressed in the words and wisdom of the first Psalm of the Bible. The psalmist describes the walk of the "blessed man" as one whose "delight is in the law of the Lord" and characteristic of the one who "meditates day and night" in God's Word or law (Psalms 1:1, 2).

Disciples who remain faithful to the end will have the honor of hearing Jesus say to them, "Well done, good and faithful servant... enter into the joy of your lord" (Matthew 25:21). May that be said of you. Amen.

> All authority has been given to Me in heaven and on earth. Go therefore and make disciples of all the nations, baptizing them in the name of the Father and of the Son and of the Holy Spirit, teaching them to observe all things that I have commanded you; and lo, I am with you always, even to the end of the age. Amen. (Matthew: 28:18-20)
>
> If you abide in My word, you are My disciples indeed. And you shall know the truth, and the truth shall make you free. (John 8:31, 32)

STEPS TO FOLLOW

Write the name of your church

_____

"Where membership is a program of discipleship"

STEP 1

✎ Complete the ABCs of Salvation (handout)

STEP 2

✎ Attend new members orientation
✎ Complete and return membership documents (handouts)

STEP 3

✎ Complete discipleship (new member) classes
✎ Submit assignments to the class facilitator

STEP 4

✎ Receive the right hand of fellowship

STEP 5

✎ Register for other discipleship classes
✎ Join and serve ministries in the church

STEP 6

✎ FRANgelize – Evangelize your Friends, Relatives, Associates, and Neighbors for Christ
  ○ Disciple others for Christ

He who began a good work in you will be faithful to complete it. (Philippians 1:6)

ABCs OF SALVATION

(To be completed by the students)

First Things First

The message of the gospel is as simple as ABC. The ABCs, however, though elementary, form the basis for all reading and writing. For sound Christian living, it is as important to learn the essential ABCs of the gospel as it is necessary to learn the rudimentary alphabet.

Complete the following:

All are guilty of sin

1. For [   ] have [   ] and fall short of the glory of God (Romans 3:23).

2. [   ] we like sheep have gone astray; we have turned, [   ], to his own way; and the Lord has laid on Him the iniquity of us [   ] (Isaiah 53:6).

3. But we are [   ] like an unclean thing, and [   ] our righteousness are like filthy rags; we [   ] fade as a leaf, and our iniquities, like the wind, have taken us away (Isaiah 64:6).

All are under condemnation

1. For the wrath of God is revealed from heaven against [   ] ungodliness and unrighteousness of men, who suppress the truth in unrighteousness (Romans 1:18).

2. For [   ] as have sinned without law will also perish without law, and [   ] as have sinned in the law will be judged by the law (Romans 2:12).

3. Therefore, just as through one man sin entered the world, and death through sin, and thus death spread to [   ] men, because [   ] sinned (Romans 5:12).

All need to be saved

1. Repent, and let every one of you be baptized in the name of Jesus Christ for the remission of sins; and you shall receive the gift of the Holy Spirit. For the promise is to you and to your children, and to [   ] who are afar off, as many as the Lord our God will call (Acts 2:38, 39).

2. I tell you no; but unless you repent you will [   ] likewise perish (Luke 13:3).

Believe that Jesus is your means of salvation

1. [   ] on the Lord Jesus Christ, and you will be saved, you and your household (Acts 16:31).

2. [   ], to them He gave the right to become [   ] of [   ], to those who [   ] on His name (John 1:12).

3. For God so loved the world that He gave His only begotten Son, that whoever [   ] in Him should not [   ] but have [   ] (John 3:16).

4. He who [   ] in the Son has [   ] life; and he who does not [   ] the Son shall not see life, but the wrath of God abides on him (John 3:36).

Confess your sins (confess means to agree with God that He is right and we are wrong)

1. If we [   ] our sins, He is faithful and just to forgive us our sins and to cleanse us from all unrighteousness (1 John 1:9).

2. If you [   ] with your mouth the Lord Jesus and believe in your heart that God has raised Him from the dead, you will be saved (Romans 10:9).

Call upon God for salvation

1. For whoever [   ] on the name of the [   ] shall be saved (Romans 10:13).

2. He shall [   ] upon Me, and I will answer him; I will be with him in trouble; I will deliver him and honor him. With long [   ] I will satisfy him, and show him My salvation (Psalm 91:15, 16).

◆

After reviewing the ABCs of salvation above, make a commitment/recommitment to the Lord affirming the truth of God's Word. Whenever doubts arise, review these ABCs. Memorize the Scriptures to assure yourself of God's unfailing promise to save and keep you from ever being lost again. Now, write down your commitment.

Submit the completed copy of UNIT IA to the teacher/facilitator for class for credit.

Complete and place in your workbook reminder section until you have finished the discipleship studies. You may also post it in a visible place as motivation to continue your discipleship training and growth. Submit a copy to the teacher/facilitator of your next class for credit.

MY DISCIPLESHIP COMMITMENT

This is to certify that on this _____
day of _____ in the year of our Lord _____
that I _____ being of sound mind,
contrite in heart, and resolute in faith do hereby submit my life to
the lordship of Jesus Christ. Therefore, I present my body to God
as a living sacrifice. I dedicate my soul to the worship of His name.
I submit my mind to be trained in the whole counsel of God as a
faithful disciple until I am able to rightly divide the Word of truth to
disciple others. Further, I commit my spirit to the fullness of the Holy
Spirit and promise to love the brethren, to always seek the salvation
of my household, my family, and all with whom I come into contact.
Recognizing that I am totally reliant on His mercy and grace, I do now
consent by my hand:

Signed _____ Date _____

DEFINING CHRISTIAN DISCIPLESHIP

Christian discipleship is:

A theologically sound mentoring process that thoroughly transforms mere believers into ardent followers of Jesus Christ.

An understanding of Christian discipleship will enhance our appreciation for the subject. Hopefully, this will lead to the serious application of the principles taught. Consequently, we will all become better disciples of Christ in our daily living. In practical terms, this means we will learn and live out the essential principles Jesus Himself taught His Apostles and to whom He gave that Great Commission:

> All authority has been given to Me in heaven and on earth. Go therefore and make disciples of all the nations, baptizing them in the name of the Father and of the Son and of the Holy Spirit, teaching them to observe all things that I have commanded you; and lo, I am with you always, even to the end of the age. Amen. (Matthew 28:18-20)

The heart of that Commission is to "make disciples." However, the challenge that arises is being involved in "teaching them to observe all things that I have commanded you." Therefore, this study of discipleship is of such importance, it can hardly be exaggerated. We should consider it a divine imperative to properly grasp what it entails.

The first step to achieving that grasp is understanding the uniqueness of the subject of Christian discipleship. As we shall see, it is not mere cognitive learning. Rather, it is rooted in spiritual actuality. The Christian disciple is someone who has been radically changed into God's active agent for making and maturing other disciples.

Some limited elaboration on the structural aspects of the working definition of Christian discipleship should prove helpful.

1.   THEOLOGICALLY SOUND

Christian discipleship is theologically sound because it is Biblical. It is the time-honored method of passing on the message of Scriptures and its commensurate life of faith in God from the fathers to the heirs of the gospel. This unbroken chain of spiritual training did not begin in the New Testament era. Rather, it is rooted in the Old Testament. Discipleship is clearly seen in the traditional father and son depiction of the prophet and his mentees.

In the Old Testament, protégées of Seers were called the sons of the prophet and the presiding prophet regarded as the father (2 Kings 2:1-12; 1 Samuel 10:1-12). In the New Testament, the same practice is evident in the ministry of Jesus, the Son of God, who called men to follow Him. He also instructed them to make disciples of all ethnic groups throughout the world (Matthew 4:18-22; 28:18-20).

One notable disciple of the apostles was the apostle Paul. He exemplified the tradition of transmitting the message from the elders (spiritual fathers) to their protégées (spiritual sons) as he ventured on missionary work throughout the Roman Empire (1 John 2:1, 12; 2 Timothy 1:1-7; Titus 1:1-5).

Timothy, in particular, whom Paul personally mentored, was regarded as his son in the gospel. Paul groomed him to function in his stead and recommended him to the Philippian church in a leadership capacity as the apostle's representative.

> But I trust in the Lord Jesus to send Timothy to you shortly, that I also may be encouraged when I know your state. For I have no one like-minded, who will sincerely care for your state. For all seek their own, not the things which are of Christ Jesus. But you know his proven character, that as a son with his father he served with me in the Gospel. Therefore, I hope to send him at once, as soon as I see how it goes with me. But I trust in the Lord that I myself shall also come shortly. (Philippians 2:19-24)

Having become as competent in the gospel as his father (Apostle Paul) in the ministry, Timothy was instructed to disciple others as he was discipled. In doing so, the process would continue in an unbroken chain of faithfulness to Christ.

> You therefore, my son, be strong in the grace that is in Christ Jesus. And the things that you have heard from me among many witnesses, commit these to faithful men who will be able to teach others also. (2 Timothy 2:1-2)

Christian discipleship, therefore, is the practice of the prophets, the Son, and in turn, His apostles, as well as those to whom they entrusted the gospel.

2. TEACHER-CENTERED MENTORING PROCESS

Christian discipleship is perhaps best characterized as a process of didactic communication from the teacher to the student who is being molded. In other words, it is teacher-centered mentoring. The dynamic interaction between the teacher and the student might also be characterized as the most effective method of instruction.

Unlike the modern Western classroom lecture format, Christian discipleship is an open-ended life-on-life process. Life-on-life is a term used in mentoring relationships in a variety of contexts. In the context of the teacher and student, it is a proven, effective method of learning that involves the teacher and student in a reciprocal teamwork dynamic. Nevertheless, there are distinctive aspects of the life-on-life concept in respect to Christian discipleship.

Generally, in a typical classroom, the instruction process is often restricted to the interplay between teacher and student(s) in a given place, space, and time. However, in Christian discipleship, ideally, the students are exposed to the full life of the teacher-mentor. They are allowed and expected to learn by directly observing the teacher's life experiences. Strengths and weaknesses, successes and failures are all learning experiences (2 Timothy 3:10).

In the ideal Christian discipleship process, the learning is more comprehensive because it goes beyond the classroom experience. Granted, such may seem risky given that teachers or mentors - however well-intentioned or principled - may let down their charges and disappoint those who look up to them. However, that very humanity is an instructive part of the discipling process from which we must not shy away. This was even true of Jesus, our ideal teacher and mentor. In His perfect humanity, the disciples observed Jesus when He was hungry, exhausted, roiling with anger, disappointed, overwhelmed, weakened, and needing help (Matthew 4:2; John 2:13-17; 4:6; Luke 17:17; 24:26).

Jesus exposed Himself to His disciples at what might be described in practical terms as the "gut level" when He shared with them His agony before facing the cross saying, "My soul is exceedingly sorrowful, even to death" (Matthew 26:38).

Therefore, in Christian discipleship, teachers and students need not be afraid of their humanity being seen as they both grow in grace and in the knowledge of the Lord. Teachers and students in the context of Christian discipleship need not focus on keeping up appearances. Instead, they should strive to follow the Lord in spite of their situations and encourage each other to do the same. Here are some examples:

- There were shortcomings in the relationships of Job and his friends who misunderstood his suffering
- The church observed Peter's failings as he observed theirs
- There was a falling out between Paul and Barnabas, his initial mentor
- Timorous Timothy had to be encouraged and schooled by Paul, his mentor

Other lapses and failures are recorded in Scripture as lessons to learn (Job; Matthew 26:69-75; Luke 24:36-41; Acts 12:12-16; 11:1-3; 15:36-40; Galatians 2:11-21; 2 Timothy 1:6, 7; Revelation 2-3).

By contrast, in a conventional classroom setting, the student may only observe the instructor within the period of instruction. Behaviors, views, and opinions expressed outside the confines of that classroom are not expected to be a part of the specific subject matter. For example, an instructor may extol the virtues of a planned economic system of government but practices an exploitive, capitalistic lifestyle outside the classroom in his regular daily living. The modern student is not expected to equate the two, that is, the socialist instruction and the capitalist instructor. The subject and the subject matter here are diametrically opposite, but hypocrisy will not necessarily be applied.

Exemplified by Christ

However, in Christian discipleship, as exemplified by Christ, the instructor and the instruction are both the subject matter. In Christian discipleship, both the teacher and that which is taught in regard to principles, laws, statutes, and ordinances are critically connected. The very practice of traditions, customs, and more become interpretive as the way they are to be lived out by the habit(s) or lifestyle of the teacher (Greek=*didaskalos*).

Hence, in Christian discipleship, the subject matter is not for mere philosophical reflection or interaction. That is why, for example, Jesus repeatedly instructed His disciples to do as He had done (John 13:12-17). Jesus, as a teacher or mentor, was always aware that He was regarded as the paradigm exemplar. Therefore, He was the one setting the standard for such relationships.

This principle was not lost on His disciples as they, in turn, exacted the same from their followers. They consistently pointed their followers to the sterling example of Christ as the one to be ultimately emulated even in the worst of circumstances (Hebrews 3:1; 12:2; 1 Peter 2:21).

Synchronization Principle

Another unique feature of Christian discipleship is the principle of the synchronization of teacher and text. In demonstrating this standard, Jesus reiterated and reaffirmed the Law. However, He emphatically steered His disciples away from its aberrations as practiced by the Pharisees and scribes (Mark 7:8-13; Matthew 15:2-6). This synchronization of the text and the teacher is seen in the profound and extensive discourse of Jesus, known popularly as the Sermon on the Mount.

In the Sermon on the Mount, Jesus exposed the gap between what teachers of the Law said and how they lived or related to their disciples. In what may be better termed, the teaching on the Mount, Jesus clarified the life of Christian discipleship for His followers by His bold punctuating declaration, "You have heard it said... but I say unto you" (Matthew 5:21, 27, 31, 33, 38, 43). Repeatedly, Jesus warned them to live as He lived and as He taught them to live – not as the world lived (Matthew 20:25-28; Luke 22:25-30). Christian discipleship does not subscribe to the philosophy of "Do as I say but not as I do." Rather, it is the seamless, singleness of His message to 'Follow Me and do as I do, and live as I live'. This is the dynamic essence of Christian discipleship. The apostle Paul powerfully expresses this same dynamic truth in these words: "Imitate me, just as I also imitate Christ" (1 Corinthians 11:1).

Furthermore, Christian discipleship is not a passive classroom experience where there is a disconnection between the teacher as a lecturer and the student as a class member. Rather, Christian discipleship is a more direct life-on-life, teaching-learning, mentoring experience between a teacher and a student in a dynamic relationship of mutual accountability.

3. THOROUGH

Christian discipleship is thorough because it is a method of instruction that encompasses, not only the teaching itself but the application of what is taught. It requires a complete, careful observance of the teachings of Christ so that education, as well as training, is in view. This is implied in the original Hebrew language usage that refers to teaching and learning: *limmud* and *malmud*.[i] These Hebrew words suggest that the disciple is prodded to do what the Lord requires as the plowman goaded oxen to accomplish his task.

Similarly, a disciple is obliged to follow the life of Christ in totality and not to select the aspects he or she prefers. Such a selective mindset is contrary or antithetical; it is counterproductive to being a Christian disciple. The Christian disciple is expected to observe all that Jesus taught. This comprehensive thoroughness of practice is expressed in the Scriptures in words that show that God requires complete devotion from those who follow Him. For example, the prophet Isaiah says this:

> Bind up the testimony, seal the law among my disciples. (Isaiah 8:16)

Nothing was to be left open to whim or fancy.

Moses also showed that God required the same devotion of the children of Israel:

> You shall not add to the word which I command you, nor take from it, that you may keep the commandments of the LORD your God which I command you. (Deuteronomy 4:2)

God required that Israel keep the commandments of the Lord with diligence and thoroughness. Likewise, true disciples are to embrace with entirety, the teachings of Christ and His apostles. Precious personal enrichment is to be gained by fully appropriating all of those teachings.

Thus, the Christian disciple has no other agenda than to follow the Lord with ardent endeavor and alert eagerness of body, soul, and mind. This total commitment will lead to the realization of what God desires in the life of the disciple. The point here is the comprehensive nature of the learning process. The approach and attitude of the Christian disciple may be likened to an apprentice who learns by observing both instruction and practice, precept and example.

---

i   As one of the twelve words for teaching in the OT, *lāmad* has the idea of training as well as educating. The training aspect can be seen in the derived term for "oxgoad," *malmēd*. In Hosea 10:11 Ephraim is taught like a heifer by a yoke and goad. The Ugaritic, *lmd* means "learn/teach" and *lamādu* means "learn" in Akkadian. The principle use of this verb is illustrated in Ps 119. Here is repeated the refrain, "Teach me thy statutes" or "thy judgments" (vv. 12, 26, 64, 66, 68, 108, 124, 135, 171). At the request of king Jehoshaphat, a group of men went out and taught the book of the Law in the cities of Judah (2 Chronicles 17:7, 9). While Greek uses two different words for "to learn" (*manthanō*) and "to teach" (*didaskō*), each having its own content, goal, and methods, Hebrew uses the same root for both words because all learning and teaching is ultimately to be found in the fear of the Lord (Deuteronomy 4:10; 14:23; 17:19; 31:12, 13). To learn this is to come to terms with the will and law of God.

Cost of Discipleship

Jesus requires His disciples to carefully count the cost of pursuing Him, inclusive of a thoughtful calculation of the losses one may incur.

> For which of you, intending to build a tower, does not sit down first and count the cost, whether he has enough to finish it…so likewise, whoever of you does not forsake all that he has cannot be My disciple. (Luke 14:28-33)

On the other hand, that thoughtful calculation should include consideration of the kingdom one will inherit.

> Everyone who has left houses or brothers or sisters or fathers or mothers or wives, or children or lands, for my name's sake, shall receive a hundredfold, and inherit eternal life. (Matthew 19:29)

Therefore, thoroughness of teaching, learning, and in living the life of Christ is a principle hallmark of Christian discipleship. It transforms the mind, body, and soul (Acts 20:27; 2:42-47; 2 Timothy 2:15; 3:16).

4. TRANSFORMATIVE

Ultimately, Christian discipleship is a transformative process. This is so because it is a dynamic learning experience that significantly alters the life of the learner. The learner develops through stages of growth – from infancy to maturity, from ignorance to reasoned understanding, from incompetence to competence, from weakness to strength, from doubt and fear to courage and faith, from moral depravity to righteousness –depending on what is being taught and who is teaching and learning.

The discipleship process is complete when the disciple is able to disciple others in the same manner he or she was discipled. Paul instructed Timothy whom he discipled.

> The things that you have heard from me among many witnesses, commit these to faithful men, who will be able to teach others also. (2 Timothy 2:2)

Clearly, Timothy graduated from mentee to mentor. Such transformation is possible because Christian discipleship is a process in which an eminent teacher (*didaskalos*) intentionally expounds and exemplifies knowledge to his students or apprentice students (*mathetes*). This is done so the students are apt to emulate that teacher in word and deed, not simply share a philosophical perspective.

Consequently, Christian discipleship requires an intimate, interdependent or symbiotic relationship between the teacher imparting his cognitive and experiential knowledge and the student imbibing and replicating that knowledge to the degree that the student becomes as learned as the teacher. Jesus says:

> It is enough for a disciple that he be like his teacher, and a servant like his master. (Matthew 10:25)

This dynamic of the student attaining the status *of the* master was demonstrated in the life and witness of the apostles.

> Now when they saw the boldness of Peter and John, and perceived that they were uneducated and untrained men, they marveled. And they realized that they had been with Jesus. (Acts 4:13)

Jesus was the Master Teacher (*Talmid*) of the Law (*Torah*) and His disciples were apprentices (*talmidim*). Twelve were called into closer association with Him. They were to be trained, commissioned, and then sent out ahead of Him to do the very works He had done.

In Luke's Gospel, we have the record of Jesus commissioning His disciples thus:

> Then He called His twelve disciples together and gave them power and authority over all demons, and to cure diseases. (Luke 9:1)

Those disciples commissioned for that special task became known as "the Twelve," a name that was used repeatedly to identify the twelve apostles.

> Then He appointed twelve, that they might be with Him and that He might send them out to preach, and to have power to heal sicknesses and to cast out demons: Simon, to whom he gave the name Peter; James the son of Zebedee and John the brother of James, to whom he gave the name Boanerges, that is, "Sons of Thunder"; Andrew, Philip, Bartholomew, Matthew, Thomas, James the son of Alphaeus, Thaddeus, Simon the Canaanite; and Judas Iscariot, who also betrayed him. (Mark 3:14-19; Matthew 26:14, 20, 47; Mark 9:35)

The radical transformation of the Twelve enabled them to set out the fundamentals of faith of the Christian church. These apostles who had started out as mere "babes" in the knowledge of God became the ones who revealed the mysteries of the gospel of the kingdom of God and His Christ. The apostle Paul explains that the foundation of the church is:

> Built upon the foundation of the apostles and prophets, Jesus Christ Himself being the chief cornerstone (Ephesians 2:20)

Female Disciples Transformed

The devoted female disciples of the Lord were also transformed. These devout women were mainly described as those who catered to the physical needs of Jesus and His apostles prior to His resurrection.

Luke tells us that many women were prominent in the service of Christ as He went through several villages preaching the glad tidings of the kingdom with the Twelve.

> Certain women who had been healed of evil spirits and infirmities – Mary, called Magdalene, out of whom had come seven demons, and Joanna, the wife of Chuza, Herod's steward, and Suzanna, and many others who provided for Him from their substance. (Luke 8:2, 3)

However, after the resurrection of Jesus, these women were chosen to be the first to report to the apostles and the rest of the disciples that they had seen the resurrected Lord.

> It was Mary Magdalene, Joanna, Mary the mother of James, and the other women with them, who told these things to the apostles…and they did not believe them. (Luke 24:10- 11)

Later, Jesus upbraided the men to whom these women delivered the news of His resurrection for their unbelief (Luke 24:22-26).

Women were also among the 120 disciples who were in the upper room on the day of Pentecost. They were there to experience the promised outpouring of the Holy Spirit upon all flesh, thereby fulfilling the prophecy of Joel.

> And it shall come to pass afterward that I will pour out My Spirit on all flesh;
> your sons and your daughters shall prophesy…and on My maidservants
> I will pour out My Spirit in those days. (Joel 2:28, 29; Acts 2:18)

Thus, mere ordinary people – men and women, fishermen, and tax collectors - were transformed by the discipleship of Rabbi Jesus. They became the foundation stones of His church of which He is the Chief Cornerstone (Ephesians 2:20; 4:11; 1 Corinthians 12:28).

Transformative Pattern

In the subsequent ministries of the apostles, the same pattern of transformation was projected wherever they made disciples. At Antioch, for example, the Gentile believers of this initially "Jewish" faith, having undergone Christian discipleship instruction by Paul and Barnabas, assembled with the church.

Luke reports that:

> For a whole year they…taught a great many people. And the disciples were first called Christians in Antioch. (Acts 11:26)

Evidently, Luke is drawing attention to the fact that a tremendous transformative effect was working itself out among the early Christians. The Antiochian disciples were recognized (whether respectfully or pejoratively) as followers of Christ Jesus of Nazareth, the exemplar of their faith.

Later in his writings, the apostle Paul instructed the Corinthian believers to be followers of him as he was a follower of Christ. In saying that, Paul was not claiming to be fully like Christ in every respect. Rather, he was saying that the character of Christ, which he exemplified, was also to be evident in those being discipled in the churches. He instructed:

> Imitate me, just as I also imitate Christ. (1 Corinthians 11:1)

In his signature epistle to the Roman believers, Paul implored them to offer up themselves as "living sacrifices" to God and not to be conformed to the worldly systems around them. He encouraged them to be transformed by the renewing of their minds. As a result, he beseeched the Roman believers to seek after the good and perfect will of God (Romans 12:1-3).

This was quite a transformation for those who were previously trapped by compulsive, sinful, bodily desires and whose carnal minds were at enmity with God in a culture that was utterly ungodly (Romans 1:18-32; 7:24-25; 8:7).

We may say, therefore, that following Christ leads to spiritual transformation - from rebel sinner to penitent believer to Christian disciple.

Conclusion

Based on the perspective on discipleship presented above, this study calls all its teachers and students to that life of faithfulness outlined, albeit in a limited way, since this is an introductory study. The principles that will be taught herein form the basic foundation on which a life of discipleship may be established. We believe that the class dynamics and the wider church fellowship will foster spiritual growth within those who submit to them. Together, these may be launching pads for discipleship in the wider church environment. Remember that Christian discipleship is the method Jesus chose to impart the most meaningful knowledge about Himself as He commanded in Matthew 28:18, 19:

- Make disciples of all men
- Baptize them in the name of the Father, and of the Son, and of the Holy Spirit
- Teach them to observe all things which I have commanded you

The practice of Christian discipleship introduces us to God's Word, eternal life, and the operation of the Holy Spirit in our lives. The Holy Spirit will guide and nurture the Word we have received from His servants to be observed in our daily living and passed on to others we encounter.

May you study to show yourselves approved unto God, a worker who does not need to be ashamed, rightly dividing the Word of Truth so that you grow in grace and in the knowledge of our Lord and Savior Jesus Christ (2 Timothy 2:15; 1 Peter 2:1-3). May we be faithful stewards of the Master as we do His will until He returns to reward us for the work He has entrusted to our hands. Amen!

Complete the following in preparation for discipleship studies and return to the teacher/facilitator

- The ABCs of Salvation
- My Discipleship Commitment

THE CALL TO DISCIPLESHIP

SCRIPTURE FOCUS

Jesus came to Galilee, preaching the Gospel of the Kingdom of God and saying, "The time is fulfilled, and the Kingdom of God is at hand. Repent and believe in the Gospel."

(Mark 1:14, 15)

PROMPTER GUIDE

In this unit of study, you will learn about the following:

1. CALL OF THE GOSPEL

2. CALL TO REPENTANCE

3. CALL TO BELIEVE

PART I ◆ UNIT A

THE GOSPEL MESSAGE

INTRODUCTION

Everyone who desires to be a follower of Christ and seeks to join a Christian church does so because of the good messages heard concerning Jesus from the Scriptures.

Like you, others may have heard the good news about Jesus and the love of God He exemplifies through various media: a sermon in a church setting, a televangelist, a friend, reading a book or an article.

By whatever means, the message received was processed in your mind as the truth, and that conviction has motivated you to respond to the good news. That good news heard is called the gospel, but what is the gospel?

1. CALL OF THE GOSPEL

- Good News (Glad Tidings) – The good news is the story of God as proclaimed primarily by Jesus Christ, His Son, to the people of the world
- Good news of the kingdom of God concerned with the salvation through Jesus Christ

2. CALL TO REPENTANCE

- Change of mind – A change of mind upon reflection of one's actions in relation to another or to something.[ii]
- Contextually, in the New Testament, repentance always refers to:
  a. Changing one's mind or purpose for the better
  b. Regretting or being sorry for a particular sinful behavior
  c. Making a complete about-face

---

ii   Vines, Ibid, pg. 525

3. CALL TO BELIEVE

a.   To have a firm conviction producing a full acknowledgement of God's revelation or truth (John 6:68)

b.   To surrender one's self to God, who is the truth (Luke 1:38; Romans 6:13; James 4:7)

c.   To behave consistently with such surrender (Hebrews 11:8)

N.B. The one who believes may not have all the facts to fully prove what is presented. However, the hearer is fully persuaded that what is heard is the truth and merits his/her sincerest acceptance and response (Hebrews 11:1).

STUDENT ACTIVITIES

—PERSONAL REFLECTION—

(see additional exercise in Appendix)

Read the story of the repentant prodigal son in Luke 15:11-32. Stop for a moment and think about any sinful behavior in your life. Think about the negative effects it is causing, has caused, or may cause in your life or in the lives of your family members and friends. Crime, violence, prejudices, suffering, diseases, persecution, war, and poverty are all largely the results of sin in one form or another.

Think about how much better our lives would be if we felt genuine sorrow for the wrongs we've committed against others and ourselves and then refrained from them. Think about how enriched our lives would become if we turn away from our sins and follow Jesus faithfully. This is the intent of the gospel message. Your discipleship begins with your repentance. You cannot be a true disciple of Jesus Christ or a bona fide member of the church until you repent of your sin(s) and believe the gospel.

MEMORY GEM   For godly sorrow produces repentance leading to salvation... (2 Corinthians 7:10)

JOURNALIZE YOUR JOURNEY

Write down meaningful insights gained and what has impacted you most in this study segment.

Blessed is the man who ... in His law he meditates day and night. (Psalm 1:1-2)

FOR FURTHER STUDY (OPTIONAL)

- Read and reflect on these texts: 2 Samuel 11, 12; Psalms 51
- Write down any questions for which you need clarification
- Submit your questions to your class teacher/facilitator in the next session

THE CALL TO DISCIPLESHIP

SCRIPTURE FOCUS

Jesus came to Galilee, preaching the Gospel of the Kingdom of God, and saying, "The time is fulfilled, and the Kingdom of God is at hand. Repent and believe in the Gospel."

(Mark 1:14, 15)

PROMPTER GUIDE

In this unit of study, you will learn about the:

1. GOSPEL OF THE KINGDOM

2. DISLOYAL SUBJECTS OF THE KINGDOM

3. HOW DID THIS COME ABOUT?

4. DIVINE INTERVENTION

5. PROCLAMATION OF THE GOSPEL OF THE KINGDOM

PART I ◆ UNIT B

THE GOSPEL OF THE KINGDOM OF GOD

INTRODUCTION: THE LORD JESUS CHRIST

The message of the gospel of the Lord Jesus Christ points us away from our sinful behaviors. At the same time, it also offers the faith to surrender to the will of a sovereign but loving God.

The submission of our lives to the rule of the God of heaven and earth is the singular, most important objective of the gospel, which Jesus preached. It is the gospel of the kingdom of God.

1. THE GOSPEL OF THE KINGDOM

- The kingdom is the domain of God (Psalms 95:1-5; 1 Timothy 1:17; Revelation 19:6)
- The kingdom is the sphere of God's sovereign rule (Psalm 95:1-7)
- The kingdom is established in every believer (Luke 17:21)

2. DISLOYAL SUBJECTS OF THE KINGDOM

- All humanity has followed the pattern of Adam and Eve's disobedience (Genesis 6:5, 6; Romans 3:10-18)
- Disobedience places humanity under satanic control (Eph.2:1-2; 2Cor 4:4, 5)
- Satan's desire is that humanity worship him instead of God (Isa. 14:12, 15; cf. Lk.4:5-8)

3. HOW DID THIS COME ABOUT?

- God's dominion was perfect in the original creation (Genesis 1:31)
- God was in a covenantal relationship with Adam and Eve (Genesis 1:26-28)
- God gave them dominion (rule) over the earth (Genesis 1:28)
- Man disobeyed the commandment of the Lord (Genesis 3:6)

- Man's dominion was diminished by God's judgment (Genesis 3:16)
- Man's habitation changed for the worse (Genesis 3:17-19)
- Man became subject to the god of this world (Ephesians 2:2)

Note: God's power is not dependent on the loyalty of any creature (angelic or human). God's rule is evident in obedience.

Note: In a natural sense, a kingdom is a territory or country subject to a monarch. The borders of these nations are the extent of their ruler's influence according to their individual laws and systems of government. The true strength of a kingdom is the loyalty of the ruler's subjects. In other words, the more loyal the subjects, the stronger the king's rule in their lives).

4. DIVINE INTERVENTION

- Man's disobedience led to death (Genesis 2:16, 17; Romans 6:23; Revelation 20:11-15)
- God sent His Son the Lord Jesus to save the world (John 3:16)
- This is why Jesus is called the Messiah, the Christ. He is the Anointed One sent by God to proclaim the good news of salvation from sin, all manner of sickness, all types of calamity, Satan's demonic control, and most of all, death (Luke 4:18)

5. PROCLAMATION OF THE GOSPEL OF THE KINGDOM

- Jesus proclaimed the gospel of the kingdom of God
- Jesus declared the restoration of God's rule
- Jesus invited all to the kingdom of God (Luke 4:42-43)

STUDENT ACTIVITIES
—PERSONAL REFLECTION—

1. The gospel is the simple yet profound message of submitting yourself to the sovereign will of God. From your perspective, how true is that statement and why would you say it is true?

2. Obedience to the gospel restores our relationship with God. How would you explain that statement to a friend?

3. Obedience to the gospel restores our relationship with each other. How exactly would you say your obedience to the gospel affects your relationship with someone with whom you are out of favor?

4. The gospel brings deliverance at last from the tyranny of sin, the Devil, and the world. Can you identify how Satan is having victory with sin in the lives of several of your friends?

MEMORY GEM

Behold, the fear [reverence and respect] of the Lord, that is wisdom, and to depart from evil is understanding.   (Job 28:28)

JOURNALIZE YOUR JOURNEY

Write down the meaningful insights gained and what has impacted you most in this study segment.

Blessed is the man who… in His law he meditates day and night. (Psalm 1:1-2)

FOR FURTHER STUDY (OPTIONAL)

✎   Read these Scriptures:

Romans 1:8-26; Ephesians 2:1-9; Colossians 1:1-23; Philippians 2:5-11; Revelation 4, 5.

✎   Write down any questions for which you need clarification. Submit them to your teacher/facilitator in your next class for helpful responses.

NOTE: Psalm 24 shows man crowned in the earth but the Lord proclaimed as the King of Glory. How do you understand these two dynamics in the context of the kingdom of God? Submit your thoughts to your teacher /facilitator in your next class.

THE CALL TO DISCIPLESHIP

Repent and believe in the gospel. (Mark 1:15b)

SCRIPTURE FOCUS

Therefore let all the house of Israel know assuredly, that God has made this Jesus, whom you crucified, both Lord and Christ.

(Acts 2:36)

PROMPTER GUIDE

In this unit of study, you will learn that:

1. JESUS IS THE LORD OF SALVATION

2. JESUS IS LORD BY HIS RESURRECTION

3. JESUS IS LORD ACCORDING TO THE SCRIPTURES

4. JESUS AS LORD IS ESSENTIAL FOR SALVATION

PART I ◆ UNIT C

THE GOSPEL OF THE LORD JESUS CHRIST

INTRODUCTION: THE LORD JESUS CHRIST

All persons who aspire to be true disciples need to recognize Jesus as their Lord to fully understand, experience, and proclaim the salvation that comes from God through Him. His status as Lord was prophesied in Scripture and demonstrated by His resurrection from the dead. Without His lordship, there is no Christian discipleship.

On the basis of His Lordship, Christ commissioned His disciples to be His apostles in His physical absence (Matthew 28:18, 19). In turn, they proclaimed Him Lord on the day of Pentecost.

The Lordship of Jesus continues to be the critical truth that all who will receive God's salvation must accept. He alone has the power to save spiritually lost souls (Acts 4:12). Entrance into the kingdom of God requires submission to His rule and reign (Psalm 2; Revelation 11:15; 20:1-6). Coming to terms with the fact that Jesus is both Lord and Christ is the crux of the matter to all who would follow Him.

1. JESUS IS THE LORD OF SALVATION

- Jesus performed miraculous signs that no ordinary man could
  - Gave sight (John 9:6-7)
  - Fed multitudes (John 6:11)
  - Healed the sick (John 5:8, 9)
  - Raised the dead (John 11:43, 44)
  - Cast out evil spirits (Luke 4:36-42)
  - Silenced hostile critics (Luke 20:26)
  - Spoke with supernatural power (Mark 4:41)
  - Chief among the signs was His resurrection from the dead by His own power (Acts 2:24; John 2:19)

2.   JESUS IS LORD AS SEEN BY HIS RESURRECTION

- Jesus rose from the dead after being buried for three days
- Jesus showed Himself to His followers 40 days after His resurrection (Acts 1:1-3)
- Jesus Christ is the one true Lord (Greek = *kurios*) of heaven and earth (Philippians 2:10)
- Jesus alone has the power to save and the right to rule

3.   JESUS IS LORD ACCORDING TO THE SCRIPTURES

- Jesus taught that He is Lord from the scriptures (Luke 24:27; 44-49)
- Jesus' apostles taught that Jesus is Lord as shown in all the scriptures (Acts 2:40; Joel 2:28; Psalm 16:8)

4.   JESUS AS LORD IS ESSENTIAL FOR SALVATION

- Salvation is possible only in His name (Acts 4:12)
- All must repent and submit to Him totally (Philippians 2:5-11; 2 Corinthians 10:5; Romans 12:1, 2)

STUDENT ACTIVITIES
—PERSONAL REFLECTION—

1. What does the concept of Lord mean to you?

2. Why did Thomas on seeing the resurrected Lord change his perception about Jesus?

3. When Thomas saw the wounds of the resurrected Lord, did he put his fingers or hands into those wounds?

4. Were Thomas and the other disciples who had the privilege of seeing the resurrected Lord more blessed than us who have not seen but have believed?

> **MEMORY GEM**
>
> Who do men say that I am?... but who do you say that I am? (Mark 8:27- 29)

JOURNALIZE YOUR JOURNEY

Write down the meaningful insights gained and what has impacted you most in this study segment.

Blessed is the man who... in His law he meditates day and night. (Psalm 1:1-2)

FOR FURTHER STUDY (OPTIONAL)

Read these three books:

- *Who Is This King of Glory* (Tony Evans, Moody)
- *The Person of Christ* (David F. Wells, Crossway Books)
- *Jesus Divine Messiah* (Robert Reymond, Presbyterian & Reformed Publishing Co.)

NOTE: Write down any questions you need clarified. Submit them to your teacher/facilitator in your next class for helpful responses.

PART I

THE CALL TO DISCIPLESHIP

God has made this Jesus ... both Lord and Christ. (Acts 2:36)

SCRIPTURE FOCUS

"Therefore let all the house of Israel know assuredly that God has made this Jesus, whom you crucified, both Lord and Christ." Now when they heard this, they were cut to the heart, and said to Peter and the rest of the apostles, "Men and brethren, what shall we do?" Then Peter said to them, "Repent, and let every one of you be baptized in the name of Jesus Christ for the remission of sins; and you shall receive the gift of the Holy Spirit." (Acts 2:36-38)

PROMPTER GUIDE

In this unit of study, you will learn about:

1. REPENTANCE (REVISITED)

2. BAPTISM (EXPOSITED)

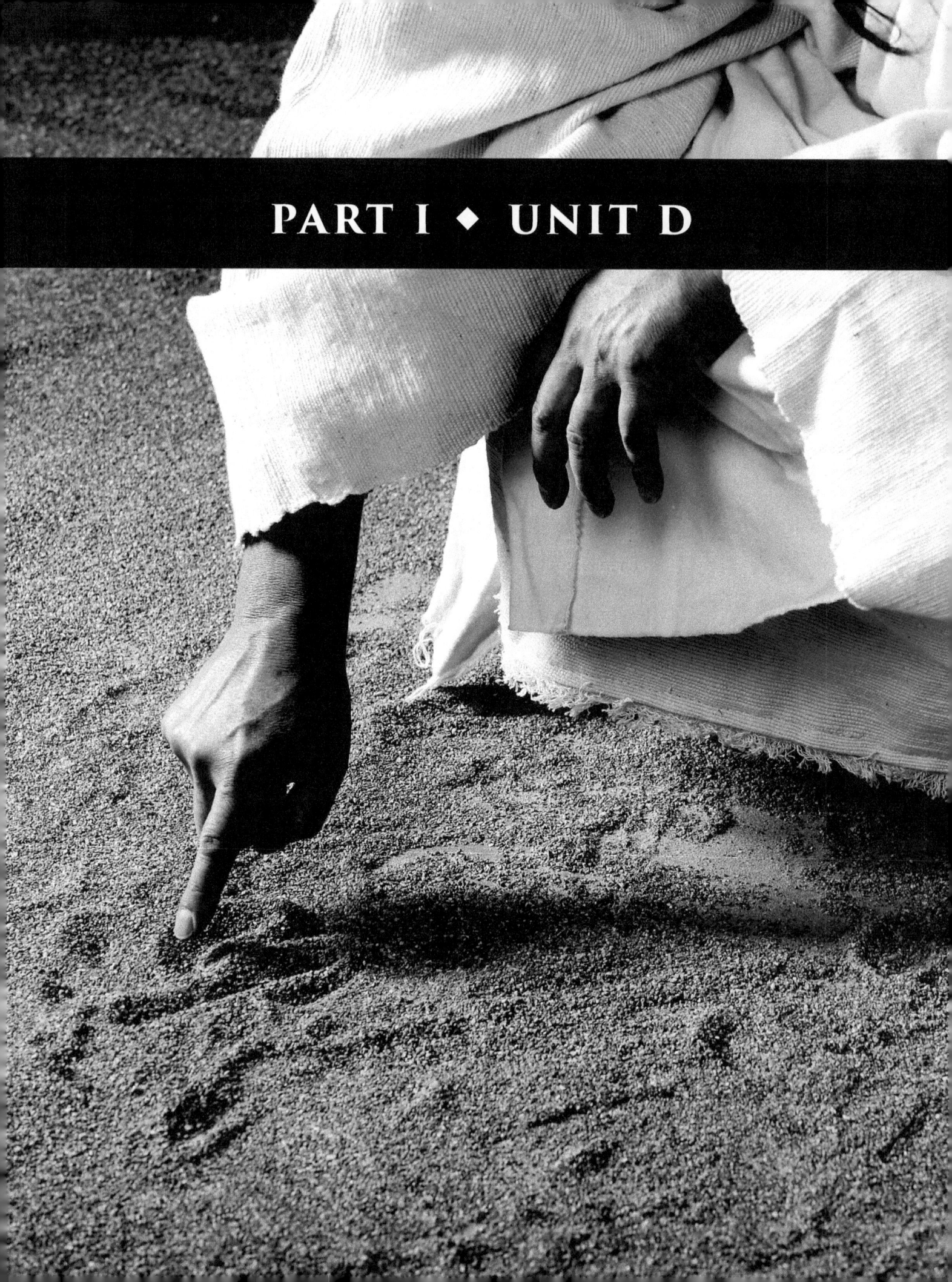

PART I ◆ UNIT D

THE GOSPEL OF JESUS CHRIST (GIFT OF SALVATION)

INTRODUCTION

Recall that the gospel is "good news" because it announces the love and favor of the King of heaven and earth to lost humans so that all may receive His salvation. That's the "good" in the good news. God was reestablishing His rule through His Son the Lord Jesus Christ.

Although God did not need to make a proclamation to assert His sovereignty, He chose to do so. He is sovereign over the entire universe. He is the Creator. All else is created by Him and, therefore, subject to His will, which He has the right to assert at any time (Psalm 24; 95; 97, 1 Timothy 1:17, Revelation 19:6).

Therefore, the proclamation of the gospel is for the benefit of those who desire to be saved from condemnation and instead to become subjects of the kingdom of heaven on earth. That's the whole point of the divine proclamation: salvation to all who would believe!

3,000 Receive Salvation!

On the day of Pentecost, the apostle Peter preached a powerful sermon to the essentially Jewish audience. In their penitent response to the disciples and Peter they asked: "Brothers, what shall we do?"

Peter's answer was swift:

> Repent and let every one of you be baptized in the name of Jesus Christ for the remission of sins; and you shall receive the gift of the Holy Spirit. For the promise is to you and to your children, and to all who are afar off, as many as the Lord our God will call. (Acts 2:38-40)

Notice that Peter's answer shows what his listeners were to "do" as an appropriate response to God's gracious offer of salvation in the face of gross transgression. They were to repent and be baptized. Let us discuss these two admonitions. The first was repentance, which was previously discussed but will be further developed here. The second, baptism, will be introduced.

1. REPENTANCE (REVISITED)

🖉   Genuine repentance moves us to do what is right

New life through the Holy Spirit was not only for those present on the day of Pentecost but to their descendants and to all who were afar off – that includes you. God's salvation is available to you. If you repent as they did, you will receive life through His name.

🖉   Genuine repentance moves us to faith in the gospel

Receiving the salvation of God is a matter of faith in the gospel on your part. Faith (Greek = *pistis*) means to be fully persuaded in one's mind that what is heard is the truth. Consequently, the believer acts upon it. Therefore, as the text above indicates, believing the gospel of salvation will involve sincere confession with our very mouths that Jesus is Lord as the gospel proclaims.

🖉   Genuine repentance moves us to ask the Lord to be saved

It is as simple as calling out to God to save us. By entreating God to rescue us, we demonstrate that we are unable to help ourselves and need Him to deliver us from our plight (Acts 2:16-21).

🖉   Genuine repentance is more than being sorry or remorseful for our sins

Repentance for the Jerusalem pilgrims translated simply into acknowledging and accepting Jesus as Savior and Lord. After presenting convincing facts, testifying, and exhorting the listeners, Peter's conclusion was clear: repent and be baptized.

Now that we have discussed repentance, let us discuss baptism.

2. BAPTISM (EXPOSITED)

a. Baptism Demonstrated

The instant decision of 3,000 "devout" Jews to be baptized by the apostles of Jesus (despised by the leaders of the people) was a remarkable demonstration of faith in the gospel. That remarkable baptism event must have been an impressive spectacle as the large group of new converts was publicly immersed in the name of Jesus, confessing Him as the Messiah.

Every new believer who accepts Jesus as Savior needs to be baptized. Understanding the significance of baptism will better equip and enable us to seek, as well as comply with this command of Jesus.

NOTE: It will not be possible to give a comprehensive treatment of the entire subject of baptism here. However, we will have a concise discussion of the principal aspects of the subject that will suffice our study and secure our obedience.

b.   Baptism Defined

The Hebrew word *ābal* (dip, plunge) in its verb form conveys the meaning of the immersion of one item into another: bread in vinegar (Ruth 2:14), feet in water (Joshua 3:15), a coat in blood (Genesis 37:31). The Greek word *baptizo* is the common Septuagint (LXX) rendering of this root.

Given that definition, it is easier to see its importance. Baptism is needed because an unclean spiritual condition makes us unfit to be in a relationship with God who is holy (Isaiah 59:1-2; Hosea 5:1-7). Sin separates the sinner from God relationally in this life and ultimately, will separate the sinner eternally (Revelation 20:11-15, 21:8; Luke13:24-27). Baptism then, is a symbol of surrender to the loving embrace of God by repentance and reception of Christ as Savior (Luke 15:20).

Baptism is not a means of salvation alone (1 Corinthians 10:1-5; 1 Peter 3:18-22)

Baptism is an act of consecration (Acts 22:16)

- Cain (Genesis 4:9-16)
- Antediluvian world (Genesis 6:1-8)
- Sodom and Gomorrah (Genesis 13:13; 18:20; 19:12-25; 2 Peter 2:70)
- Sin is a spiritual barrier (Isaiah 59:1-3)
- Sin is repulsive in nature (Isaiah 64:5, 6 cf. Ezekiel 36:25)
- Sin defiles hands and hearts (James 4:7-9)
- Sin must be cleansed so that the life is consecrated (Ezekiel 36:25)
- Baptism identifies the sinner with the sacrifice (Hebrews 9:19-22; John 13:1-11)
- Baptism Identifies the Sinner with Christ (Hebrews 9:11-15; Romans 6:4-6)

c.   Biblical Historical Cleansing

Baptism is often only seen as a New Testament concept. However, as an act of cleansing and consecration, it may be traced throughout the Old Testament. A review of it may reinforce our understanding and help us appreciate Jesus' mandate to all who will follow Him (Matthew 28:19).

- Consecration by water (Exodus 19:10, 14)
- Rite of purification (Numbers 19:20; Psalm 51:2, 7; Isaiah 1:16; Ezekiel 36:24-29)
  - At Pentecost (Acts 2:38; cf. 22:16)
  - Apostolic teaching (Acts 3:19; cf. Matthew 3:1-8; 2 Corinthians 7:1)

d.   Baptism, a symbol of spiritual cleansing

- ○   Word of God (Psalm 119:47; Ephesians 5:25-27; John 15:3;17:17; James 1:21, 22)

- ○   Blood of Jesus (Hebrews 9:11-14; 1 John 1:7-9; Revelation 1:4, 5; 7:13, 14).

- ○   Cleansing by the Spirit (Ezekiel 36:24-29; Mark 1:8; Acts 1:5, 19:1-6; 1 Corinthians 12:13; Galatians 3:27)

N.B. Earlier in our definition of baptism, we indicated that it harkens back to the immersing of garments in dyes. The makers of fine garments dipped the clothing of their clients into their color solutions to beautify them. They were irrevocably changed, especially when they were dipped in red/scarlet. Similarly, when we are baptized as sincere believers calling upon the name of the Lord for salvation, we are spiritually dipped in the blood of Christ to be irrevocably changed from sinners to saints.

STUDENT ACTIVITIES
—PERSONAL REFLECTION—

1. How important is baptism in your discipleship process?

2. What parts of the body are recommended for cleansing in the Scriptures above?

3. How does the writer recommend that those parts of the body be cleansed?

4. What importance does God put on cleanliness?

5. You have heard the saying, "Cleanliness is next to godliness." What do you suppose it means?

💡 **MEMORY GEM**

And now why are you waiting? Arise and be baptized, and wash away your sins, calling on the name of the Lord.   (Acts 22:16)

JOURNALIZE YOUR JOURNEY

Write down the meaningful insights gained and what has impacted you most in this study segment.

> Blessed is the man who… in His law he meditates day and night. (Psalm 1:1-2)

FOR FURTHER STUDY (OPTIONAL)

Review the scriptures mentioned under Baptism Symbols listed above and study their contexts. Envision the need for cleansing in a very physical sense as the case for purification is presented. John, who baptized by water, declared that Jesus would baptize with fire and the Holy Ghost. What do you suppose he meant? How is baptism, in Paul's teaching, portrayed as a form of death? (Romans 6:3-12; Colossians 2:12-15).

NOTE: Write down any questions for which you need clarification. Submit them to your teacher/facilitator in the next class for helpful responses.

DELINEATING
DISCIPLESHIP

PART II

THE CALL TO FELLOWSHIP

They continued steadfastly in the apostles'
doctrine and fellowship. (Acts 2:42)

SCRIPTURE FOCUS

Then those who gladly received his word
were baptized; and that day about three
thousand souls were added to them. And
they continued steadfastly in the apostles'
doctrine and fellowship, in the breaking of
bread, and in prayers.   (Acts 2:41, 42)

PROMPTER GUIDE

In this unit of study, you will learn about the first converts to Christianity and how:

1. **THEY CONTINUED STEADFASTLY IN THE APOSTOLIC DOCTRINE**

2. **THEY CONTINUED STEADFASTLY IN THE FELLOWSHIP OF THE APOSTLES AND DISCIPLES**

3. **THEY CONTINUED STEADFASTLY IN PRAYER WITH THE APOSTLES AND DISCIPLES**

4. **THEY CONTINUED STEADFASTLY IN CORPORATE WORSHIP**

PART II ◆ UNIT A

JOINING THE CHURCH (GREEK = *KOINONIA*)

INTRODUCTION

Joining the church is more than being among the 'saved folk' or placing your name on the church roll. To be added to the number is to become a part of the body of Christ. In common church talk, this is referred to as being 'in fellowship'.

The idea of "fellowship" refers to the common association of persons who share the same ideas, concepts, concerns, and enterprises. The term also alludes to the participating in activities as comrades who share mutual love and personal relationships with each other. Such Christian companionship constitutes a church body – the body of Christ.

Collectively, the members become a local Christian community of disciples learning how to live lovingly toward each other. This is done under the leadership of the local and general assembly of church members whom the apostle Paul called saints.

> To the church of God which is at Corinth, to those who are sanctified in Christ Jesus, called to be saints, with all who in every place call on the name of Jesus Christ our Lord, both theirs and ours. (1 Corinthians 1:2)

For Christian fellowship to occur, each person who joins the church needs to be discipled. Remember, a disciple is an adherent, a devoted student or follower whose aim is to become like his teacher.

Thus, when we submit ourselves to sound biblical instruction among the believers, we will be transformed from our carnal selves and conformed to the very image of Jesus Christ.

1. THEY CONTINUED STEADFASTLY IN THE APOSTOLIC DOCTRINE

It was clear from Peter's message that there was much the new believers needed to understand. Therefore, they became:

- Adherents – they stuck to the apostles' teachings and instructions

- Avid – they continued faithfully in their attendance
- Ardent – they gave unremitting care to the admonition
- Audacious – they persevered in faith without fainting

2. THEY CONTINUED IN THE FELLOWSHIP OF THE APOSTLES AND DISCIPLES

- They recognized that the apostles and the other followers were disciples of Jesus
- They were the recipients of the Spirit of God and not others such as the Sadducees, chief priests, or elders
- They broke bread together from house to house
- They had all things in common; they sold and shared their possessions
- They gave to the needy among them (Acts 2:45; 4:34-37)
- They had singleness of heart i.e. sincerity and simplicity
- They had joy; they were extremely jubilant (exultant)

N.B. To be in fellowship (Greek = *Koinonia*) means to share in common; to be a partaker; one who contributes or communicates as a partner. Therefore, they became the disciples of the apostles in the same way that the apostles had been the disciples of Jesus three years prior.

3. THEY CONTINUED IN PRAYER WITH THE APOSTLES AND DISCIPLES

- Prayer was made in the same manner as the apostles (Acts 3:1; 6:4)
- Prayer was made in each other's houses (Acts 2:46; 12:5, 12)
- Prayer was made for boldness to continue witnessing (Acts 4:23-33)
- Prayer was made for divine assistance (Acts 4:23-33)
- Prayer was made for the deliverance of their leaders (Acts 12:5-17)
- Prayer was made for forgiveness of their persecutors (Acts 7:59, 60)

4. THEY CONTINUED IN CORPORATE WORSHIP

- They attended temple services (Acts 2: 46)
- They praised God publicly and had favor with the people (Acts 2:47)

- They ate together in fellowship meals (Jude 12; 1 Peter 2:13)
- They sang psalms, hymns, and spiritual songs (Acts 16:25)
- They read Scripture (1 Timothy 4:13; Luke 4:16; 10:26; Acts 13:15; Romans 15:4)
- They exhorted and were exhorted (Acts 17:1-2, 10, 11)

STUDENT ACTIVITIES
—PERSONAL REFLECTION—

Study and meditate on the following scriptures pertaining to the church and answer the following questions? (Matthew 16:18; 18:15-20; Ephesians 5:21-32; Acts 13:1-3; Revelation 1).

1. How significant is your church assembly to the Lord?

2. How significant should your church assembly be to you?

3. What role did the church have in your conversion?

4. What role do you envision for yourself as a member of this church assembly?

MEMORY GEM

Now, therefore, you are no longer strangers and foreigners, but fellow citizens with the saints and members of the household of God, having been built on the foundation of the apostles and prophets, Jesus Christ Himself being the chief cornerstone, in whom the whole building, being fitted together, grows into a holy temple in the Lord, in whom you also are being built together for a dwelling place of God in the Spirit.

(Ephesians 2:19-22)

JOURNALIZE YOUR JOURNEY

Write down the meaningful insights gained and what has impacted you most in this study segment.

Blessed is the man who … in his law he meditates day and night. (Psalm 1:1-2)

FOR FURTHER STUDY (OPTIONAL)

Read:

- *The Community of the King* (Howard Snyder, IVP)
- *Jesus Divine Messiah* (Robert Reymond, Presbyterian & Reformed Publishing Co.)
- Review the Hymn "The Church's One Foundation"
- Research the Nicene Creed

NOTE: Write down any questions for which you need clarification. Submit them to your teacher/facilitator in the next class for helpful responses.

PART II

THE CALL TO FELLOWSHIP

And the Lord added to the church daily those who were being saved. (Acts 2:47b)

SCRIPTURE FOCUS

Then those who gladly received his word were baptized; and that day about three thousand souls were added to them ... And the Lord added to the church daily those who were being saved. (Acts 2:41, 47b)

PROMPTER GUIDE

In this unit of study, you will learn about the character of the church:

1. **THE BODY OF CHRIST**

2. **THE TEMPLE OF GOD**

3. **THE FLOCK OF GOD**

4. **THE BRIDE OF CHRIST**

5. **THE CALLED OUT PEOPLE OF GOD (GREEK = *EKKLESIA*)**

JOINING THE CHURCH FELLOWSHIP (Greek = *KOINONIA*)

INTRODUCTION

It is God's will that all who receive His Son Jesus Christ as Savior and Lord are united in fellowship as one body, members of one another. Having then accepted the Lord Jesus Christ as Savior, it is necessary to be in fellowship with fellow believers. Collectively, all believers in Jesus Christ are called the church. They make up the body of Christ and the kingdom of God on earth. Every new believer becomes part of the family of God by virtue of the new birth. This rather mystical union has implications for the individual believer, as well as the collective body of believers. On the one hand, new members have the personal responsibility to maintain a conscientious relationship of sharing, caring, and participating in the church assembly they joined. They also need to submit themselves to the leadership of those appointed in the assembly they have joined.

On the other hand, the church leadership has the responsibility of discipling new members helping them fit into the structure and ministries of the local assembly. This was and is the practice of the Christian church from its inception. Therefore, an understanding of the biblical structure of the church is essential during the discipleship process so we can have a comprehensive view of its composition, function, and purpose. In this discipleship segment, we will examine these descriptions given in Scripture against the backdrop of our text, which is considered the birth of the Christian church.

Believers Baptized and Added

- The joining of the initial 3,000 believers was a conscientious, bold, dramatic decision underscored by their public baptism
- The new converts were "devout Jews" who had come from several nations to celebrate the Feast of Pentecost (first fruits) in Jerusalem (Exodus 23:16; 34:22-23; Leviticus 23:9-21)
- They heard and understood the gospel of Jesus Christ; they were pricked in their hearts
- They united themselves with the apostles and the saints who proclaimed the gospel

- More believers were added daily. 5,000 more were added a few days later; then the number multiplied (Acts 2:47; 4:4; 6:1). This was exponential growth
- There was no Christian church building to enter as we do today
- There was no established institution with formal offices: pastors, bishops, elders, ushers or even deacons initially
- The assembly of believers who were followers of Jesus the Christ became the early church for distinction

1.   THE BODY OF CHRIST

- Body of individual believers united and connected to each other
- Body of related members functioning together
- Body of member parts that are interdependent on each other
- Body spiritually integrated as in a physical body (Romans 12:5)
- Body of members mutually concerned about each other (1 Corinthians 12:14-23)
- Body that should be without schisms (1 Corinthians 1:10-13; Romans 6:15; 12:5)
- Body of individual responsibility for each believer (Ephesians 4:11-16)
- Body of contributing members (Ephesians 4:11-16)
- Body that maintains the righteous nature of Christ (1 Corinthians 6:15)
- Body with Christ as her preeminent head (Colossians 1:18)

2.   TEMPLE OF GOD/BUILDING

- God's house – the house of the great King (Hebrew = *Hêkāl*, Psalm 11:4; Micah 1:2; Habakkuk 2:20; Isaiah 6:1)
- God's place to meet with His people (Numbers 9:15; 3:1-15; Psalm 24; 15; 46:1-4; Zechariah 6:12, 13; John 2:12-17; Mark 11:15-17)
- God's place of worship and encounter (Exodus 25:8, 22; 1 Samuel 1:4-9)
- God's presence is manifested there (Exodus 13:21; 28:30; 30:1-6; Leviticus 16:20; 1 Samuel 28:6)
- God's physical presence experienced in Jesus (John 1:14)
- God's people are the true temple, not the stones and other physical materials that house them (Matthew 18:18; 23:37; Luke 23:34-36; 1 Corinthians 5:4)
- God's Spirit inhabits His temple (Ephesians 2:19-22)

- God's living temple is made up of individual living stones (believers)
- Built upon the foundation of the apostles and prophets, with Christ as the Chief Cornerstone (1 Peter 2:4, 5; cf. Ephesians 2:19-20)

3. THE FLOCK OF GOD

- Each believer is one of God's beloved sheep (Psalm 23; 95:7)
- All believers are God's flock (Psalm 77:20; 78:52; 80:1)
- God is their Shepherd (Psalm 79:13; 95:7; 100:3)
- Jesus is the Good Shepherd who protects His Father's sheep (John 10:6)
- Jesus is the Chief Shepherd of the church flock (1 Peter 5:4)
- God will judge all who mistreat His sheep (Jeremiah 23; 50:6; Ezekiel 34; Zechariah 13; Matthew 9:36)
- God appoints pastors (under-shepherds) over their care (1 Peter 5:2; Psalm 77:20; 80:1)
- God's flock will stand at His right hand when He comes to judge the nations (Matthew 25:31-34)

4. BRIDE OF CHRIST

- His beloved bride (Ephesians 5:21-33; Song of Solomon)
- His betrothed bride (2 Corinthians 11:2; Matthew 25:1-13)
- He is her bridegroom (Matthew 9:15; 25:1-13; John 3:29; Revelation 21; 22:16-21; Song of Solomon)

5. CHURCH OF GOD (GREEK = EKKLESIA — CALLED OUT ASSEMBLY)

- The assembly called from the world (Acts 2:39; Romans 8:30)
- The Lord adds those who are being saved (Acts 2:47; 5:14)
- The Lord appoints, chooses, and elects all who would be saved (Isaiah 42:1; Acts 9:15; Romans 8:28-32; 1 Peter 2:4-10; Revelation 17:14)
- The Lord accepted and led you here as He did those on the day of Pentecost

STUDENT ACTIVITIES
—PERSONAL REFLECTION—

Each disciple is groomed to live out faith in a specific sociological and religious context. Therefore, it is important that attention is paid to the structure and culture of the specific assembly/denomination you choose to join. This is so you may become part of the brethren in compliance with the particular rules and regulations that govern the church. This is no different from what happened in the early church. As it grew in scope and size, various principles and practices were put in place as Scripture and the leading of the Holy Spirit allowed (Acts 6; 11:19-30; 15).

As new assemblies were planted throughout the Greco-Roman world, epistles were written with spiritual and temporal instructions so that the membership lived in harmony without inviting any blasphemy to the name of Christ. Matters such as idolatry, eating foods offered to idols, sexual behaviors, marriage, family, circumcision, the Holy Spirit, governmental authority, master and slave relationships, and a myriad of other issues were all addressed in the epistles of the apostles and their designates. We are privileged to have these writings to guide our current assemblies, especially those in peculiar circumstances. Care must be taken to learn the manners of your church context so as to be a vital part of the body of Christ there.

Reflect on the hymn "The Church's One Foundation" (Samuel J. Stone; Samuel Wesley)

The Church's One Foundation

The church's one foundation is Jesus Christ her Lord; she is his new creation by water and the Word. From heaven he came and sought her to be his holy bride; with his own blood he bought her, and for her life he died.

Elect from every nation, yet one o'er all the earth; her charter of salvation, one Lord, one faith, one birth; one holy name she blesses, partakes one holy food, and to one hope she presses, with every grace endued.

Though with a scornful wonder we see her sore oppressed, by schisms rent asunder, by heresies distressed, yet saints their watch are keeping; their cry goes up, "How long?" And soon the night of weeping shall be the morn of song.

Mid toil and tribulation, and tumult of her war, she waits the consummation of peace forevermore; till, with the vision glorious, her longing eyes are blest, and the great church victorious shall be the church at rest.

Yet, she on earth hath union with God the Three in One, and mystic sweet communion with those whose rest is won. O happy ones and holy! Lord, give us grace that we like them, the meek and lowly, on high may dwell with thee.

Answer the following questions:

1. What images studied do you see in the first stanza?

2. According to the second stanza, how is the church composed?

3. How is the unity of the church hinted in the same stanza?

4. According to the third stanza, what are the two threats to the church's unity?

MEMORY GEM

Now, therefore, you are no longer strangers and foreigners, but fellow citizens with the saints and members of the household of God, having been built on the foundation of the apostles and prophets, Jesus Christ Himself being the chief cornerstone, in whom the whole building, being fitted together, grows into a holy temple in the Lord, in whom you also are being built together for a dwelling place of God in the Spirit. (Ephesians 2:19-22)

JOURNALIZE YOUR JOURNEY

Write down the meaningful insights gained and what has impacted you most in this study segment.

Blessed is the man who... in His law he meditates day and night. (Psalm 1:1-2)

FOR FURTHER STUDY (OPTIONAL)

- Meditate on Revelation 1-3
- Read *The Church in the Bible and the in World*, Carson D.A., Wipf & Stock Publishers

NOTE: Write down any questions you need clarified. Submit them to your teacher/facilitator in the next class for helpful responses.

PART II

THE CALL TO FELLOWSHIP

You shall receive the gift of the Holy Spirit (Acts 2:38b).

SCRIPTURE FOCUS

And you shall receive the gift of the Holy Spirit. For the promise is to you and to your children, and to all who are afar off, as many as the Lord our God will call. (Acts 2:38b,39)

Therefore being exalted to the right hand of God, and having received from the Father the promise of the Holy Spirit, He poured out this which you now see and hear. (Acts 2:33)

PROMPTER GUIDE

In this unit of study, you will learn about:

1. **OUTPOURING OF THE HOLY SPIRIT**

2. **THE GIFT OF THE HOLY SPIRIT- THE SPIRIT OF GOD**

3. **THE DAY OF THE LORD- AT PENTECOST?**

4. **THE HAND OF THE LORD**

PART II ◆ UNIT C

THE GIFT OF THE HOLY SPIRIT

INTRODUCTION

Earlier in our study, we examined the principal thrust of Peter's charismatic message – Jesus Christ is Lord. We also learned that submission to His lordship as evidenced by repentance and baptism is necessary for our salvation. More importantly, however, Peter also declared that those who would repent and are baptized in the name of the Lord Jesus will receive the "gift of the Holy Spirit." He was reminding his fellow Israelites and the Gentile converts to Judaism present that the charismata of the Holy Spirit is exactly what God had promised to bestow on all flesh – those present, their children, and all those who are afar off – "as many as the Lord our God will call." (Acts 2:39)

These words are as significant to us today as they were to those present in the primary Pentecostal audience. This was so due to the fact that what was apparent to them that day was prophetic. It foretold what needs to be a present reality in our lives today – the gift of God's grace in the person of the Holy Spirit. He is God's promise to us as well. We are "those who were afar off" (Ephesians 2:11-14; Romans 10:11-13). We are among the "many" whom the Lord our God has called to salvation (Ephesians 4:1-7).

To appreciate the immeasurable worth of the gift of the Holy Spirit, we need to review its value to those on whom it was first bestowed at Pentecost, and then to believers in the New Testament church in the age of the Holy Spirit. It is the essential gift itself that makes endowments of spiritual gifts to each believer possible.

1. THE OUTPOURING OF THE HOLY SPIRIT — A TIME OF REFRESHING

- A time of refreshing
- A sign of great significance
- Each people group present heard their distinct native dialect
- Peter stood up and explained the significance of the phenomenon
- The Holy Spirit was poured out as prophesied by Joel (Acts 2:17-21 cf. Joel 2:28-32)
- The Holy Spirit was the gracious gift of God received upon repentance and baptism in the name of the Lord Jesus Christ

2.   THE GIFT OF THE HOLY SPIRIT — THE SPIRIT OF GOD

- The Holy Spirit is the Spirit of God in the Old Testament

- The Holy Spirit endowed with the abiding presence and power of God

- Every priest, prophet, and king was anointed as a sign of their functioning under the aegis and authority of the Spirit of God

- The absence of the Spirit of God meant divine rejection (1 Samuel 18:1-12; 28:5; Psalm 51:11)

- The Holy Spirit inspired the prophetic writings (Isaiah 11:1-2; 63:10, 11, 14; Ezekiel 3:12, 14; Micah 3:8; Zechariah 4:6; 2 Peter 1:16-21)

- Even Gentile nations recognized the supremacy and presence of the Holy Spirit (Numbers 24:1-13; Daniel 4:8, 9)

3.   THE DAY OF THE LORD — AT PENTECOST?

- As prophesied, it was a day of renewal for all Israel

- The Holy Spirit would be poured out on male and female, young and old

- Such a glorious phenomenon would occur on "the day of the Lord," a special time of judgment on the enemies of Israel

- A time of God's people returning to Him with fasting and weeping rending their hearts

- A time of new grain, new wine, new oil

- A time of salvation for all who call upon the name of the Lord

- Peter made it clear that day had come at Pentecost (Acts 2:14-16)

- He called the devout Jews gathered in Jerusalem to salvation in the name of the Lord Jesus Christ

- To participate in the outpouring of the gift of the Holy Spirit

- To refuse would be a tragic rejection that could only invite the judgment of God envisioned by Joel and reiterated by Peter

- To save themselves from their corrupt generation (Acts 2:16-21 cf. Hebrews 1:1-2; 3; 4)

4.   THE HAND OF THE LORD

- Evidence of the presence of the Holy Spirit in the lives of believers (Acts 4:31, 33; 6:3, 8-10; 7:54-56; 8; 9:17-18; 10:44-48; 11:21-24; 13:1-3; 19:1-7)

- It is essential, therefore, that we recognize the person, presence, and the power of the Holy Spirit in our lives as disciples of Christ

- He regenerates, illuminates, baptizes, empowers, indwells, and equips the believer with spiritual gifts for acts of service. Let us study these aspects of the Holy Spirit:

  a. Regenerating Spirit

    > The Holy Spirit is the One who regenerates each believer

    > To enter the kingdom of God one has to be born of "water and of the Spirit"

    > Regeneration is spiritual birth

    > It is essential for any to enter the kingdom of God

    > Regeneration is mysteriously done by the Spirit (John 3:8)

    > The Holy Spirit convicts of sin, of righteousness, and of judgment to come in respect of Christ (John 16:8-11)

    > On the day of Pentecost, the Holy Spirit pricked the hearts of the crowd leading them to submit to Jesus as their Lord and Christ.

  b. Illuminating Spirit of Truth

    > He illuminates the carnal mind to the light of the gospel of Jesus Christ

    > He is the Helper sent alongside the believer to bring the realization of the truth about Jesus (John 14:16; 15:26, 27; 16:13-14)

    > He gives insight into the truth about God and to understand the message of the gospel of Jesus Christ, which appears as foolishness (2 Corinthians 4:3,4)

    > He enables the natural mind to comprehend the spiritual mysteries of God's grace (1 Corinthians 2:6-16)

    > He draws all to the Father through His dynamic influence (John 6:44)

    > He gives spiritual discernment of the scriptures (1 Peter 1:21; 1 Corinthians 2:14).

  c. Baptized by the Spirit

    > It is the Spirit of God who baptizes the believer into the body of Christ (1 Corinthians 12:13)

N.B. We have already explored the concept of baptism in the previous study. It was noted that water baptism is a sign of the baptism of the Holy Spirit (see pg. 49), which is in view here. The unregenerate human nature is renewed in the image of God from all sinful desires and behaviors. This is done by the washing or renewal of the Holy Spirit, which is poured out on us generously through Jesus Christ our Lord (Titus 3:3-7).

Notice based on Paul's letter to Titus:

The unregenerate state before salvation

- Foolish
- Disobedient
- Deceived
- Slaves to lust and sinful pleasures
- Malice
- Envy
- Hatred

The grace of God shown in Christ

- Kindness
- Love of God our Savior
- Mercy
- Salvation
- Justification
- Hope of eternal life
- Heirs

The regenerating work of the Holy Spirit

- Washing
- Regenerating
- Renewal

The Holy Spirit is presented here in the act of baptism. He is "poured out" on us abundantly through Jesus Christ our Savior (Titus 3:6). The imagery used here is the same as that in respect of water baptism, which is indicative of the fact that one is a visible representation of the other. As believers are enjoined into the local body by water baptism, they are simultaneously joined to the mystical body of Jesus Christ by the Holy Spirit. The believer is rendered dead to the world and born again by the regeneration of the Spirit. Therefore, the believer is free to be united with Christ (Romans 6:5; 7:1-6).

    d. Baptized with Power

        o Believers are endowed with power to serve the kingdom of God. Jesus' disciples were endued with power from on high – the power of the Holy Spirit:

            i. Exousia power to be effective eyewitnesses of the truth about the Lord Jesus Christ (Acts 1:5,8)

      ii. Dunamis (dynamite) power to blast away the lies, hypocrisies, and stony-hearted resistance of the Sanhedrin, Pharisees, chief priests, and elders (Matthew 28:11-15; Luke 4:28, 29-36)

      iii. Kratos power to withstand the steely hegemony of Rome

      iv. Ischus power to overcome their fears to face temperamental crowds and antagonistic leaders (Acts 2; 4:9-12; 5:27-32; 7; 9:19-25; 13:50; 14:1-7, 19)

- The indwelling presence of the Holy Spirit led to unlikely converts among the priests, Samaritans, persecutors, and Gentiles at large (Acts 6:7; 8; 9:17-19; 10, 11).

- Every Christian needs the power of the Holy Spirit to confront similar challenges.

e. Indwelling Spirit of God

- The Holy Spirit is the gift of God's very presence in the life of the believer

- The presence of God tabernacled with the people in the wilderness in route to the Promised Land

- The Spirit of God abides in the lives of believers individually and collectively as they make their spiritual journey to the new Jerusalem (Hebrews 11:13-16; 12:22-29; Revelation 20:1-4)

- The Holy Spirit resides in the body temple of the believer filling him/her with His divine presence (1 Corinthians 6:17-20; 3:16-17; 8:11)

- Believers are to be filled with the Spirit exhorting each other in psalms, hymns, and spiritual songs as did the sons of Korah (1 Chronicles 6:31-48; 16; 15:17-22; Ephesians 5:19)

- Believers are not to grieve the Holy Spirit or quench His holy flame because of irreverent, carnal behaviors (1 Corinthians 6:9-11; Ephesians 4:30)

- Believers are to renew their minds and be transformed into the image of Jesus Christ (Romans 12:1-8).

f. He gives gifts to believers

- The Holy Spirit Himself gives gifts (charismata) to each believer He indwells (1 Corinthians 12-14; Romans 12:1-8; Ephesians 4:1-16)

- This special endowment of grace demonstrates the Spirit's presence and operation in the lives of the believer

- The gifts equip them to serve the body of Christ and the world at large

- These spiritual abilities are not for self-aggrandizement but rather, for the glory of God (1 Corinthians 14:20-40; 1 Corinthians 13:1-3; Acts 8:9-24) o   As a result, the church achieves unity in the faith, in the knowledge of the sons of God, and maturity in the fullness of Christ

o   It is important to be aware of what gifts you have been endowed with to be better able to function as a Spirit-filled member of the body of Christ.

STUDENT ACTIVITIES
—PERSONAL REFLECTION—

The significance of the Holy Spirit in your life as a believer in Jesus Christ cannot be overstated. The Holy Spirit is to be understood as fundamentally essential for us to be saved, to be a part of God's family, and to live in accordance with His will. We cannot even pray appropriately without the agency of the Holy Spirit because it is He who gives assurance of our salvation. He intercedes on our behalf as we petition God our Father in the name of Jesus (Romans 8:26). Failure to be conscious of His abiding presence will result in carnal, unchristian behaviors that will result in God's chastisement and even death (1 Corinthians 5:1-6; 11:27-30; Hebrews 12:5-13).

How aware are you of the Spirit's presence in your life? Your body is to be presented to God daily as a living sacrifice, holy and acceptable to Him. "This is your reasonable service." You are no longer to conform to this world but to be transformed by the renewing of your mind (Romans 8:5-17). In this way, you will manifest the gift(s) with which He will endow you to evidence what is that good and perfect will of God (Romans 12:1-4).

MEMORY GEM

In whom also, having believed, you were sealed by the Holy Spirit of promise, who is the guarantee of our inheritance until the redemption of the purchased possession, to the praise of His glory. (Ephesians 1:13b-14)

JOURNALIZE YOUR JOURNEY

Write down the meaningful insights gained and what has impacted you most in this study segment.

Blessed is the man who… in His law he meditates day and night. (Psalm 1:1-2)

FOR FURTHER STUDY (OPTIONAL)

- Meditate on John 14:25, 26; 15:26, 27; 16:7-15
- Read:
  - *Institutes of the Christian Religion* (Book 1), Calvin, John
  - *The Holy Spirit*, Walvoord, John F, (Zondervan)
  - *The Holy Spirit*, Fergusson, Sinclair B. (IVP)
  - *The Holy Spirit in the Old Testament*, Pink, Arthur (Philadelphia, Fortress)
  - *The Holy Spirit in the New Testament*, Sweete, Henry (London, MacMillan)
  - *Christian Theology*, Erikson, Millard, (Baker pp. 845-883)

NOTE: Write down any questions you need clarified. Submit them to your teacher/facilitator in the next class for helpful responses.

THE CALL TO FELLOWSHIP

The whole body, joined and knit together by what every joint supplies.
(Ephesians 4:16)

SCRIPTURE FOCUS

From whom the whole body, joined and knitted together by what every joint supplies, according to the effective working by which each part does its share, causes growth of the body for the edifying of itself in love.

(Ephesians 4:16)

PROMPTER GUIDE

In this unit of study, you will learn about:

1. **SPIRITUAL GIFTS (GREEK = *CHARISMATA*)**

2. **THE SPIRIT, THE GIVER**

3. **THE GIFTS**

4. **PURPOSE OF THE GIFTS**

5. **USE OF SPIRITUAL GIFTS TODAY**

6. **SUMMARY**

PART II ◆ UNIT D

THE GIFTS OF THE HOLY SPIRIT

INTRODUCTION

In the previous study, we examined how new members are assimilated into the body and how they are discipled by those whom the Lord set over His work. We also studied how the disciples fellowshipped together as a community of believers committed to each other's welfare and wellbeing. Such cohesiveness was possible because of the concerted efforts of all who contributed.

Some persons such as Barnabas seemed to have an extra special ability to show love and concern over and above the ordinary. Others tried to duplicate his qualities but without the sincerity with which he shared his personal possessions; the results were disastrous. Others, like Stephen and Phillip, were able to perform miracles, as well as articulate the Word of God powerfully and with clarity. It is clear that several people were given supernatural abilities to do amazing things (Acts 5:12-16; 6:8; 4:35-37; 8:4-8).

Who gave them these abilities and why? Did they have a choice as to what abilities they could have? What was the purpose of these extraordinary, spiritual abilities? Were those dynamic abilities only for those we read about in the Bible? Do Christians today experience the same charismatic phenomenon? All these questions will be explored in this study segment as we examine the functions of each member of the body then and now.

1.   SPIRITUAL GIFTS (GREEK = *CHARISMATA*)

Recall from our prior study that the church is presented as a body and every member is a part of the body. In the physical body, each cell, organ, tissue, tendon, muscle, and bone performs unique, individual, physiological functions. Similarly, each believer is equipped to serve the church in special, individual, spiritual ways for the benefit of all. These special abilities to serve each other are called charismata-spiritual gifts. These are unique endowments that are granted without merit on the part of the recipients by which they can exhibit extraordinary powers. Therefore, it is essential that all believers are aware of the gift(s) with which they have been endowed (1 Corinthians 12:1, 4-11).

2. THE SPIRIT, THE GIVER

The supernatural abilities that were exhibited first by the apostles and then by those who joined them were imparted by the Holy Spirit just as Jesus had promised:

> And being assembled together with them, He commanded them not to depart from Jerusalem, but to wait for the Promise of the Father "which", He said, "you have heard from Me; for John truly baptized you with water, but you shall be baptized with the Holy Spirit not many days from now." (Acts 1:4-5)

> You shall receive power when the Holy Spirit has come upon you; and you shall be witnesses to Me in Jerusalem, and in all Judea and Samaria, and to the end of the earth. (Acts 1:8)

Jesus called the empowering of the apostles a "baptism." They were to be enveloped with supernatural strength to proclaim Jesus Christ as Lord and Savior. John had baptized with water; the Messiah was going to baptize with the Holy Spirit and fire (Matthew 3:11).

That is exactly what happened on the day of Pentecost as the disciples waited in the upper room:

> And suddenly there came a sound from heaven, as of a rushing mighty wind, and it filled the whole house where they were sitting. Then there appeared to them divided tongues, as of fire, and one sat upon each of them. And they were all filled with the Holy Spirit and began to speak with other tongues, as the Spirit gave them utterance. (Acts 2:2-4)

- The Holy Spirit filled the disciples
- The Holy Spirit enabled them to speak in eloquent and "elevated discourse"
- The crowd that knew them to be mere Galileans was amazed
- Peter explained that it was as a result of the outpouring of the Holy Spirit in fulfillment of the prophecy of Joel (Acts 2:16 cf. Joel 2:28-29)

In the days following, other supernatural gifts were displayed:

- Healing of the sick and infirmed (Acts 3:7, 8; 5:15-16)
- Exorcism of devils (Acts 5:16; 8:7)
- Signs and wonders (Acts 5:12)
- Word of wisdom (Acts 7; 4:8-13)
- Word of knowledge (Acts 8:35)
- Resurrection (Acts 9:40)

Many more signs and wonders were done by the apostles and disciples

- The power of the Holy Spirit was working through them (Acts 5:12)

- Later in his epistle to the Corinthians, Paul reiterated this fact. He instructed that "There are diversities of gifts, but the same Spirit." (1 Corinthians 12:4)

- The Holy Spirit is the One who determines and distributes the gifts (1 Corinthians 12:4-11)

- The Holy Spirit is the sole administrator and dispenser of the gifts to believers

- All the spiritual activities, manifestations, and ministries are under the purview and by the prerogative of the Holy Spirit (1 Corinthians 12:4-7)

A Choice of Gifts

The Holy Spirit determines which gifts are to be used in any given situation. Jesus described Him as the Spirit of truth that would:

- Indwell

- Guide

- Teach

- Empower the believers in His absence so that they could bear effective testimony of Him

- He would convict the world of sin, of righteousness, and of judgment to come (John 14:16, 17; 15:6, 27; 16:7-15)

- He endows the believers to function according to the divine purpose

Signs and wonders were done to validate the apostles of Jesus (Acts 5:12). The church expanded from Jerusalem to Samaria.

- The superiority of the name of Jesus Christ was demonstrated

- Samaritans were delivered from satanic spells imposed by Simon the sorcerer resulting in great joy (Acts 8:4-12)

- Subsequently, the dead were raised and sight was restored

- The church became a force that could not be stopped or refuted in spite of deadly threats and suffering (Acts 4:31; 5:17-42; 6:8-10; 9:20-22; 10:44-48;11:19-26; 13:44-52; 14; 16)

- By the power of the Word of God they "turned the world upside down" (Acts 17:6)

- Spiritual gifts were sought and exercised in love so that the church and the world at large may be edified and saved (Acts 4:29, 30; 13:1, 2 cf. 1 Corinthians 14:1-5)

All the gifts of the Spirit need to be understood so that they may be fully utilized to achieve the will of God in the world.

3.   THE GIFTS

a.   **The Word of Wisdom** — Godly wisdom is evidenced in speech and concepts that convey the requisites for Godly living; it is the ability to give sound counsel that may draw from the divine revelation of the hidden or complex so as to make good decisions that glorify God.

b.   **The Word of Knowledge** — Divine insight that allows one to understand the inexplicable. It is an acute ability to think with an extraordinary depth and to offer counsel that expresses profound reasoning.

c.   **Faith** — A deep, resolute assurance and confidence in God and His Word as true and sure. An unwavering conviction of the truth of God's existence and of His Lordship over all people, all things, in all places, in all ages, and in eternity. It is the simple but absolute trust in God's Word as communicated through the Scriptures. Thus, the one endowed with faith will act in total expectation of the fulfillment of the Scriptures.

d.   **Healing** — The supernatural ability to remedy a malady or to restore soundness to any diseased condition (Matthew 9:1-8; Luke 9:1). Recovery of health may occur by the declaration of the healer or by the application of care (James 5:13-16; John 9:7).

e.   **Working of Miracles** — The supernatural exertion of power to produce an unlikely outcome. The supernatural exhibition of signs revealing the operation of God's activity in the natural affairs of humanity.

f.   **Prophecy** — From *pro-pheme* (Greek); to speak forth divine truth pertaining to the behavior of people in relation to the scripture, the kingdom of God, and His mandates as articulated by Christ. Consequently, the prophet may admonish, reprove, and comfort; prophet/prophetess may also predict future events and reveal the hidden, especially as it relates to the kingdom of God and the triumphant return of Christ.

g.   **Discerning of Spirits** — The inspired ability to judge between godly and ungodly spirits. It is the capacity to distinguish between those spirits that confess to the Lordship of Christ and those that promote its denial.

h.   **Various tongues (languages)** — The different distinct languages and dialects spoken by the different people groups throughout the world. While it is normal to speak in one's native tongue/dialects, it is less natural for one to have the ability to speak in a foreign language to which one has not been exposed or educated. God created the language barrier and it is by His Spirit that He gives some the ability to overcome it and to communicate across it (Genesis 11:1, 5-8; Acts 2:4-8). In his epistle to the Corinthians, Paul hints at tongues of angels, which if spoken, would be unknown unless interpreted (1 Corinthians 13:1 cf. 2 Corinthians 12:3-4)

i.   **Interpretation of tongues** — Supernatural ability to understand and translate what is said in the different distinct languages and dialects spoken by the different people groups throughout the world and possibly by angels. The interpreter is given the ability to penetrate the language barrier and travel mentally and linguistically between the two.

j.   **Service (ministering)** — Those who are willing to follow the commands of others in the proclamation and promotion of the gospel; the charitable acts of those who render Christian affection, especially to the poor and other disadvantaged groups.

k.   **Teaching** — The enhanced ability to impart instruction in a clear and precise manner so that those taught are able to grasp difficult/complex concepts. In respect of the Christian church, it is the endowment of the Spirit to instruct disciples in doctrines expounding, explaining, and instilling the mysterious, which is obscure and inaccessible to the natural mind (Acts 11:26; 8:26-35; Mark 1:21; John 7:14; Matthew 7:29; Ephesians 1:8-10; 3:2-5; Colossians 1:25-27; 1 Corinthians 2:1-14).

l.   **Exhortation** — A special form of instruction that encourages, comforts, strengthens, and entreats another that may most often be discouraged, and distressed by adversity and misfortune. The exhorter comes alongside the individual to offer consolation.

m.   **Giving** — The spiritual motivation to impart something beneficial to someone else from one's own resources; to furnish or supply what is lacking or needed whether it is requested or recognized; to contribute one's care and well being. While giving is a general act, those specially endowed with this grace are distinguished by their extraordinary, unpretentious, selfless generosity. There is an openness of heart and hand.

n.   **Administration** — The extraordinary grace to assume and discharge responsibilities diligently and earnestly. This gift enables the establishment of systems, structures, and processes that make for greater efficiency and effectiveness. It facilitates the governance, leading and direction of people and organizations. It allows for those who are qualified to preside over business affairs to set up the foundational framework upon which to build the work.

o.   **Mercy** — The exceptional ability to show kindness to the miserable and the afflicted with deep compassion. It may manifest as the assumption of or the identification with the plight of another induced by the Holy Spirit such that one is moved to action to address the pain or problem. It is evidenced by deep compassion for the suffering of others (e.g. Mother Teresa).

4. PURPOSE OF THE GIFTS

- Each gift as described is for a specific use
- Self-absorption in one's gift can cause you to lose sight of its central purpose
- Misuse of gifts can lead to confusion and disorder in the church
- Any physical cell that acts out of sync with the overall function of the body causes disease
- Any believer acting selfishly creates discord and dysfunction (1 Corinthians 14:26-33)

As Paul explained to the Ephesian believers, the gifts are dispensed so that:

- Each member may supply his/her contribution to the overall body in love
- There is synergy, unity, effective growth, and maturity (Ephesians 4:16)
- The purposes of God who has called us are accomplished
- God is glorified by redemption through the blood of Jesus to all who believe
- Jesus Christ will become the preeminent head of all creation
- The power and glory of God over heaven and earth is demonstrated (Ephesians 1:7, 20-23)
- Jesus is also the head of the church (Ephesians 4:15)

The effective exercise of the spiritual gifts by each believer as in the book of Acts will lead to the establishment of the kingdom of God on the earth with Christ as its sovereign head.

5. USE OF SPIRITUAL GIFTS TODAY

If over 2000 years ago when Peter preached it was considered the commencement of the "last days," then certainly, we are in the age of the outpouring of the Spirit even more so. Therefore, we may conclude that:

- The gifts are as relevant now as then
- Until Jesus comes, they must function as instituted
- The gifts are needed to overcome every obstacle with which it is presented (Revelation 2:7, 11, 17, 26:3, 5, 12, 21; 21:1-4)
- Without the power of the Holy Spirit, the church is powerless; individual believers will live defeated lives
- Each believer must walk worthy of his/her calling in the unity of the Spirit

6. SUMMARY

- Each believer is called and chosen to be part of the kingdom of the Lord Jesus Christ

- Each believer has been endowed with spiritual gifts through which God may achieve His purpose of salvation to all mankind

- Each believer is to exercise the spiritual endowments to the praise and glory of His name

- Each believer becomes a co-laborer with God making disciples of every ethnicity throughout the world

- Each believer is to develop and utilize the gift(s) in love

- The church will be edified, equipped, and empowered to accomplish the will of God in Christ Jesus (Ephesians 4:7-16)

STUDENT ACTIVITIES
—PERSONAL REFLECTION—

Imagine being a heart. Your task is to pump the life-giving blood to every cell that will die without your effort. All 100 trillion estimated cells need to receive the precious oxygen that comes from the lungs. Each needs the nutrients that were digested in the stomach. At the same time, each cell needs to rid itself of the toxins generated by cellular activity. Your task is to expand and contract repeatedly at the necessary rate of demand in a multiplicity of different processes, functions, and systems so that the body may be kept alive. Think how unselfishly the heart performs its task from conception to cessation. Take a quiet moment and listen to your heart. Could you be as dedicated without the excuses and selfish motivations that hinder your service?

MEMORY GEM

💡

But earnestly desire the best gifts. And yet I show to you a more excellent way.
(1 Corinthians 12:31)

Though I speak with the tongues of men and of angels, but have not love, I have become sounding brass or a clanging cymbal. And though I have the gift of prophecy, and understand all mysteries and all knowledge, and though I have all faith, so that I could remove mountains, but have not love, I am nothing. And though I bestow all my goods to feed the poor, and though I give my body to be burned, but have not love, it profits me nothing.
(1 Corinthians 13:1-3)

JOURNALIZE YOUR JOURNEY

Write down the meaningful insights gained and what has impacted you most in this study segment.

Blessed is the man who… in His law he meditates day and night. (Psalm 1:1-2)

FOR FURTHER STUDY (OPTIONAL)

- *The Holy Spirit*, Walvoord, John F, (Zondervan)
- *The Holy Spirit*, Fergusson, Sinclair B. (IVP)
- *The Holy Spirit in the Old Testament*, Pink, Arthur (Philadelphia, Fortress)
- *The Holy Spirit in the New Testament*, Sweete, Henry (London, MacMillan)

NOTE: Write down any questions you need clarified. Submit them to your teacher/facilitator in the next class for helpful responses.

DEVELOPING
DISCIPLES

PART III

THE CALL TO STEWARDSHIP

Let each one give as he purposes in his heart. (2 Corinthians 9:7a)

SCRIPTURE FOCUS

Nor was there anyone among them any who lacked; for all who were possessors of lands or houses sold them, and brought the proceeds of the things that were sold, and laid them at the apostles' feet; and they distributed to each as anyone had need. (Acts 4:34, 35)

So let each one give as he purposes in his heart, not grudgingly or of necessity; for God loves a cheerful giver. (2 Corinthians 9:7)

PROMPTER GUIDE

In this unit of study, you will learn about personal responsibility in the local church in respect of:

1. **TITHES AND OFFERING**

2. **WHAT IS TITHING?**

3. **GIVING IN THE NEW TESTAMENT CHURCH**

4. **GIVING TIME**

5. **GIVING TALENTS (PARTICIPATING IN MINISTRY)**

PART III ◆ UNIT A

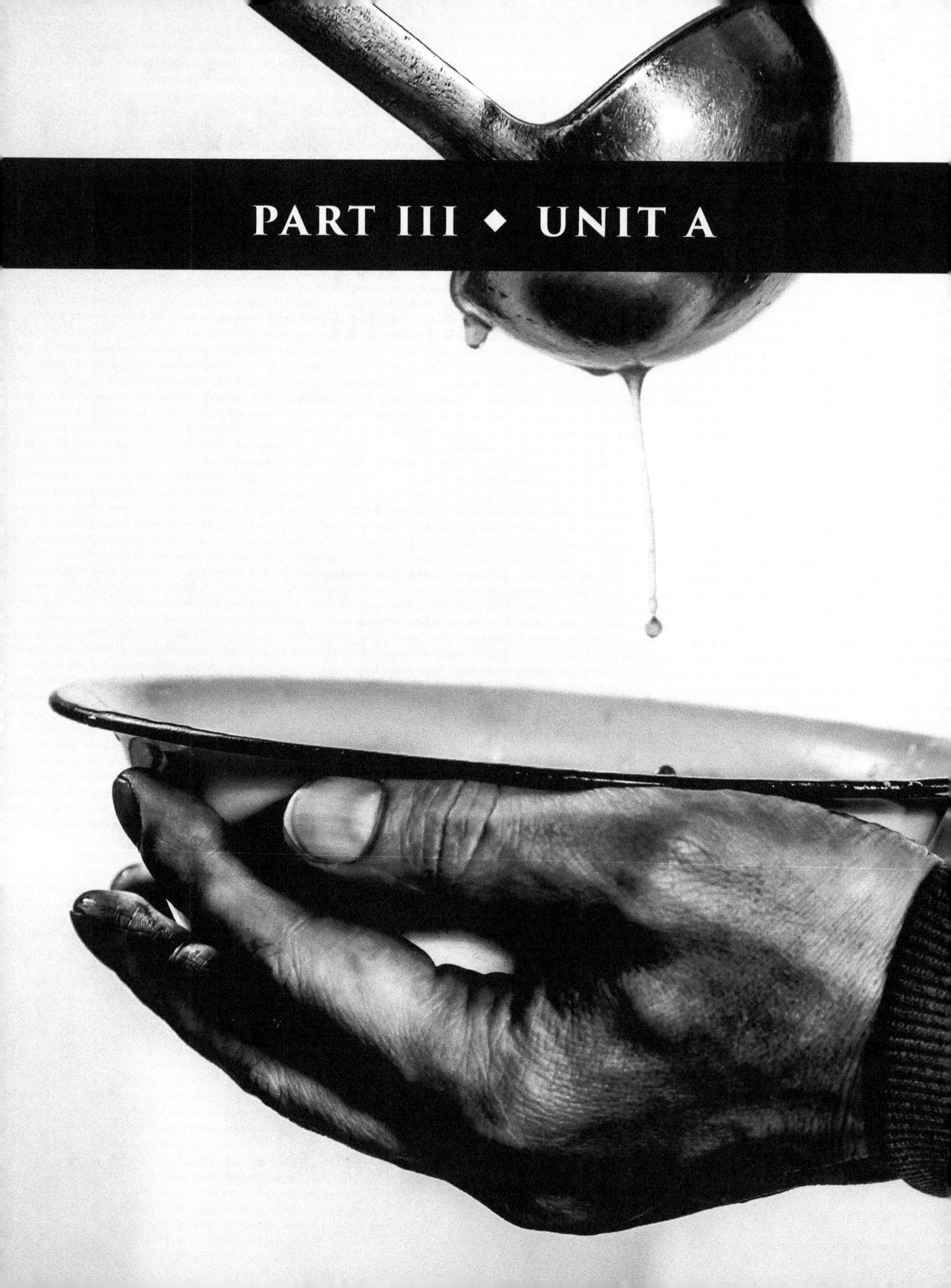

STEWARDSHIP IN THE LOCAL CHURCH

INTRODUCTION

As we continue to learn how to be disciples of Jesus Christ, it is necessary to look, not only at the spiritual contributions we make to the assembly to which we may belong, but we must also consider the tangible, personal contribution of our resources to the church organization. This is necessary so that its operations, projects, and programs are resourced for the further discipleship of others and ourselves.

As can be seen from the above scriptures, giving monetary gifts for the maintenance and welfare of the church was one of the vital signs of Christian love and brotherhood in the early church. As the church grew in spiritual power and size, many were prompted to share their material wealth so that the needs of other brothers and sisters could be met. This level of self-sacrifice was extraordinary. However, giving was not unusual given that to this point, the church was still largely Jewish and the giving of tithes and offerings to the temple for the maintenance of the priest, the Levites, the poor, and even the stranger (non-Israelites) was part and parcel of their socio-religious life (Deuteronomy 26:12; Nehemiah 10:37-39).

It was natural for the apostles, those overseeing the ministry to give gifts as acts of worship to benefit others in need much the same way such gifts were given to the priests, Levites, and prophets (Acts 4:35-37 cf. 1 Samuel 9:7, 8).

But how did this practice develop as the church incorporated the Gentiles across the Greco-Roman world? What were the practices and precepts of the apostles and church leaders on the matter as they discipled those who joined the body in the emerging new congregations in Samaria, Antioch, Rome, Corinth, Ephesus, Galatia, and so on?

A more contemporary question we need to consider is how do we give today in keeping with the faith we have inherited in the churches where we now worship? These are the questions this study segment will discuss to offer some clarity on the issue. While this unit cannot give a full treatment to each of these questions, it is hoped that it will stimulate discussion in the context of the unique church tradition in which the discussion is held and that it will lead to responsible stewardship of our time, talents, and treasure.

1.   TITHES AND OFFERING

The subject of contributing resources to a local church ministry (especially monetary donations) commonly called 'tithes and offerings' has become a controversial one in the modern Christian church largely because of two principal issues:

- The misuse and the abuse of monetary donations by the unscrupulous
- Whether Christians should be giving tithes at all, as was done under the Old Covenant.

On the one side, there are those who say that tithing is an Old Testament practice that ought not to be continued in the New Testament church of Christ. That it is part of the Law; therefore, it is no longer binding on the church. On the other side, are those who maintain that it is a valid principle that carried over into the apostolic era. Hence, it is part and parcel of the obligation of Christians to the ministry and the kingdom of Christ. How can these divergent views be reconciled? Perhaps what is needed is a primary understanding of some key terms:

a.   What is tithing?

b.   To whom were tithes given/are tithes to be given?

c.   Why were/are they given?

d.   When were/are they to be given?

e.   Where were/are they given?

Hopefully, by answering these basic questions, it will be possible to understand the issue better and determine the best course of action for the believer. It is necessary to point out that the issue of tithing cannot be discussed without reference to the complementary act of the giving of offerings as well.

2.   WHAT IS TITHING?

- A tenth part, 10%
- 10 is an ancient number for the collective whole
- In antiquity, a tenth (a tithe) was given as tribute (tax) to kings, rulers, priests, and other authorities
- It preceded the Law of Moses in which regulations for the giving and receiving of tithes and offerings were specified
- Giving tithes and offerings is also mentioned in the New Testament era in the post Law dispensation
- The modern metric system is divided into units of tens

The metric system is decimal, in the sense that all multiples and submultiples of the base units are factors or powers of ten of the unit. Fractions of a unit are not used formally. The practical benefits of a decimal system are such that it has been used to replace other non-decimal systems outside the metric system of measurements, e.g. currencies.

Historical Biblical Review:

- Tithing in the Patriarchal Period
- Abraham (Genesis 14:18-19)

The first mention of tithing is in Genesis14:20 where the Patriarch Abraham paid tithes to Melchizedek. This primary reference is pivotal in understanding the entire concept of tithing and giving:

a. Abraham paid the tithes to Melchizedek

b. Melchizedek was priest of the Most High God, king of Salem (Jerusalem), king of peace, king of righteousness (Melchizedek) (Genesis 14:18 cf. Hebrews 7:1-7)

c. His priesthood predated the Aaronic, which was given the charge of the receipt and distribution of tithes and offerings from the people of Israel

d. Melchizedek blessed Abraham who paid him the tithe of the spoils he had captured

e. Abraham tithed to Melchizedek out of reverential respect, not out of any obligation, as say a tax or tribute

f. Abraham did so as an act of worship and accepted the blessings of Melchizedek

g. Abraham refused the offer of Bera, king of Sodom to keep portions of the spoils

h. His perspective of wealth was rooted in God's provision, not man's worldly possessions

- Jacob (Genesis 28:22)

a. The Lord revealed Himself as the Lord God of Abraham and the God of Isaac to Jacob in a dream

b. The Lord promised him the land he was sleeping on

c. His descendants will be innumerable

d. God would be with him. He will keep him. He will bring him back to that very land, and that He will not leave him until all he was promised is performed

e. In response, Jacob vowed that if the Lord be with him, keep him, feed and clothe him, and return him to his father's house in peace then:

1. The Lord will be his God

2. The memorial stone he anointed and erected will be God's house

3. He will give back a tenth to the Lord, of all that He gives.

✎ Tithing Under the Mosaic Law

a. The tithes were for the maintenance and upkeep of the Levites

b. The Levites of the tribe of Levi were separated by the Lord to be priests to the rest of the nation of Israel

c. They were not given tribal land allotments but small homesteads and cities

d. The lack of land allotments would leave the Levites deprived of the means of food cultivation and production

e. Tithes and offerings were to maintain the Levites (Leviticus 27:30-34; Numbers 18)

f. Disadvantaged groups such as the stranger, the fatherless, and widows were also to be recipients of tithes that were to be made available for their free usage (Deuteronomy 14:22-29; 18:1-8).

✎ Observations

Several Bible scholars offer insights into the system of tithing as practiced under the Law. Two of their perspectives on tithing help us to appreciate its divine intent and its human benefit:

1. According to Dennis Writ-Lind, tithing had primary and secondary benefits in the Israelite community and "refers to justice, mercy, and faithfulness." Justice to the Levites, mercy to the poor, and faithfulness to God (cf. Matthew 23:33).

2. J.B. Payne in Theology of the Older Testament describes tithing in two ways:

a. Godward – He expresses that it was not onerous but a joyful act of worship to the Lord (Deuteronomy 12:12, 28 cf. 1 Corinthians 9:7). He also sees it as a display of submission and dependence (2 Chronicles 31:1-5).

b. Manward – It maintained community life and fostered the inter-relatedness of the people of God. It allowed for the Levites (deprived, disadvantaged) to be ministered to by the people whose labors and produce were given in tithes to them. The third-year tithe provided for the poor, especially orphans and widows, "the proverbial subjects of neglect…a major step towards a healthy society."

✎ Tithing and Giving in the Post Law New Testament Period

a. Tithing was still in place during the earthly ministry of Christ (Matthew 23:23)

b. It is mentioned in His parable about the vain prayer of the Pharisee and the publican (Luke 18:12)

c. The writer of the Hebrews uses the paying of tithes to demonstrate the superiority of the priesthood of Jesus Christ to that of the Aaronic

d. Christ is portrayed as receiving tithes from Aaron (the lesser to the greater)

3. GIVING IN THE NEW TESTAMENT CHURCH

- Jesus was apparently open to receiving the offerings of those who showed Him generosity and kindness

- He received monetary gifts from women for His ministry (Luke 8:1-4; John 12:5, 6)

- He also authorized His apostles to receive gifts when they went forth ministering as He dispatched them (Luke 10:7; Matthew 10:42)

- It was natural, therefore, for the apostles to receive the gifts of the church for the furtherance of the gospel (Acts 2:45; 4:32-37; 6:1-2)

- Monetary aid was collected for one cause or another as the gospel spread into the Greco-Roman world

- Church members were expected to share their possessions with each other in structured and organized ways, as well as on an individual basis motivated by love (1 Corinthians 16:1; 2 Corinthians 8)

Note the principal words used:

- Liberality

- Ministry to the saints

- Grace

- Giving of self

- Love

- The example of Christ

- Equality

- Abundance

- Honesty

- Diligence

- Observations

  a. Giving was to be of free will and a ministry (service) to others

  b. It was to be seen as a grace, a special spiritual endowment of the Spirit, which enables generosity to be shown

  c. It was a selflessness and expression of love that gives of one's abundance to restore equality among the body in honesty and diligence

  d. It draws on the example of Christ who divested Himself of all His heavenly riches to enrich us who are blessed as a result with every spiritual blessing (Ephesians 1:1-7)

e.   Unlike the traditional tithe (10%), Christ gave His all (100%)

f.   Giving in the New Testament is not limited to a tenth but unlimited by love

g.   Giving was to meet the needs of the brethren

h.   Giving was to be done cheerfully

i.   The giver was not simply meeting a physical need, but was also maintaining the witness of the gospel. It supported the Church, in distress, in Jerusalem where the apostles were headquartered and the missions of the apostle Paul into the Greco-Roman world, in particular (Acts 10:28-30; 15:1-4; Philippians 4:15-23)

4.   GIVING TIME

Giving to the local church must not only be seen in financial terms. Most churches can only function with the voluntary help of many who give of their valuable time. Many churches have elaborate and extensive programs that cater to youth: camps, VBS, mentoring, sports and after-school activities. Others have television and cable broadcasts reaching many via satellite and the internet. Then there are missions (local and overseas), evangelism, and community outreach offering food, clothing, and shelter to the disadvantaged and the poor. Counseling for individuals, couples, and families are also faith-based programs that can be found in the portfolio of many churches.

All these ministries require funding, administrating, managing, and staffing by people who voluntarily give themselves in service to help others. Often, they do so even after completing their own day jobs and at the expense of their other interests and obligations. Spending time in the service of Christ is an invaluable gift that results in souls being saved and Christian enrichment (Acts 11:22-26; 14:3, 26-28; Philippians 2:25-30; Romans 16).

5.   GIVING TALENTS (PARTICIPATING IN MINISTRY)

Time is not all that is required of church members. Merely attending a church program is not enough. Spectating is not the most productive activity. Thus, many also give the church their talents. Most ministries are staffed by people who have excellent skills and competencies that are used to earn significant incomes in the secular world but are often lent to the cause of the kingdom gratis.

For example, the multi-media ministries of most churches have personnel who are equally competent to their counterparts in the secular media houses. However, they choose to utilize their lucrative skills for the cause of Christ. Likewise, many secular artists will pale in comparison to the vocal and musical abilities of those who minister in the hallowed halls of the churches far and away from the spotlights and stages of the world. Yet, these gifted musicians are pleased to overlook the lure of Tinsel town and Broadway for the sheer joy of glorifying God in their assemblies.

As a matter of fact, many accomplished secular artists developed their talents in churches or borrowed their genres of music from sacred halls. In other areas, accountants, human resource personnel, administrators, teachers, lawyers, financial advisors, builders, and countless other professionals can all be found busily toiling in the service of Christ. The scriptures are filled with examples of such persons who enriched the church with their skills. Many of them recognized they were equipped by God to so minister to His people (1 Chronicles 16; 25; Exodus 35:30-35).

What natural gift(s) and competencies do you have that may be used to advance the work of the church? What needs have you identified in the local assembly or global church body that you would like to see met? What spiritual gifts do you have or desire to have that could build up others and contribute to the development of the kingdom of God?

STUDENT ACTIVITIES
—PERSONAL REFLECTION—

- How were you evangelized by the church?
- How well was its message delivered to you?
- Were you well received by the brethren when you made the decision to follow Christ?
- What is your perception of the discipleship program, which is designed to help you grow?
- What weaknesses and strengths do you see that may be improved?
- What threats exist that could limit growth and progress?
- Do you see opportunities that could be capitalized on?
- What irks or irritates you when you see it done poorly or not at all?

All these questions may be used to provoke you to become an active, contributing member of the body of Christ exactly as the Spirit of God intended. Remember that you are a steward of the gifts, talents, and resources with which you have been blessed so you can be a blessing to others.

> **MEMORY GEM**
>
> Every good gift and every perfect gift is from above, and comes down from the Father of lights, with whom there is no variation or shadow of turning.   (James 1:17)

JOURNALIZE YOUR JOURNEY

Write down the meaningful insights gained and what has impacted you most in this study segment.

Blessed is the man who … in His law he meditates day and night. (Psalm 1:1-2)

FOR FURTHER STUDY (OPTIONAL)

- *Giving and Tithing*, Burkett, Larry (Moody Publishers, 1998)
- *Beyond the Collection Plate*, Durral, Michael (Abingdon Press)
- *Did the Apostle Paul Teach Tithing to the Church?* Kithcart, Jonathan (Winepress Publishing, 2001)
- *The Cycle of Victorious Giving: Your Time, Your Talent, Your Treasure*, Stan and Linda Toler (Beacon Hill Press)

THE CALL TO STEWARDSHIP

Let each one give according as he purposes in his heart.
(2 Corinthians 9:7a)

SCRIPTURE FOCUS

Abide in Me, and I in you. As the branch cannot bear fruit of itself, unless it abides in the vine, neither can you, unless you abide in Me. I am the vine, you are the branches. He who abides in Me, and I in him, bears much fruit; for without Me you can do nothing.　　(John 15:4, 5)

PROMPTER GUIDE

In this unit of study, you will learn about personal responsibility in the local church.

1. PRINCIPLES TO LIVE BY

A. QUIET TIME WITH GOD

B. TELL SOMEONE WHAT THE LORD HAS DONE FOR YOU

PART III ◆ UNIT B

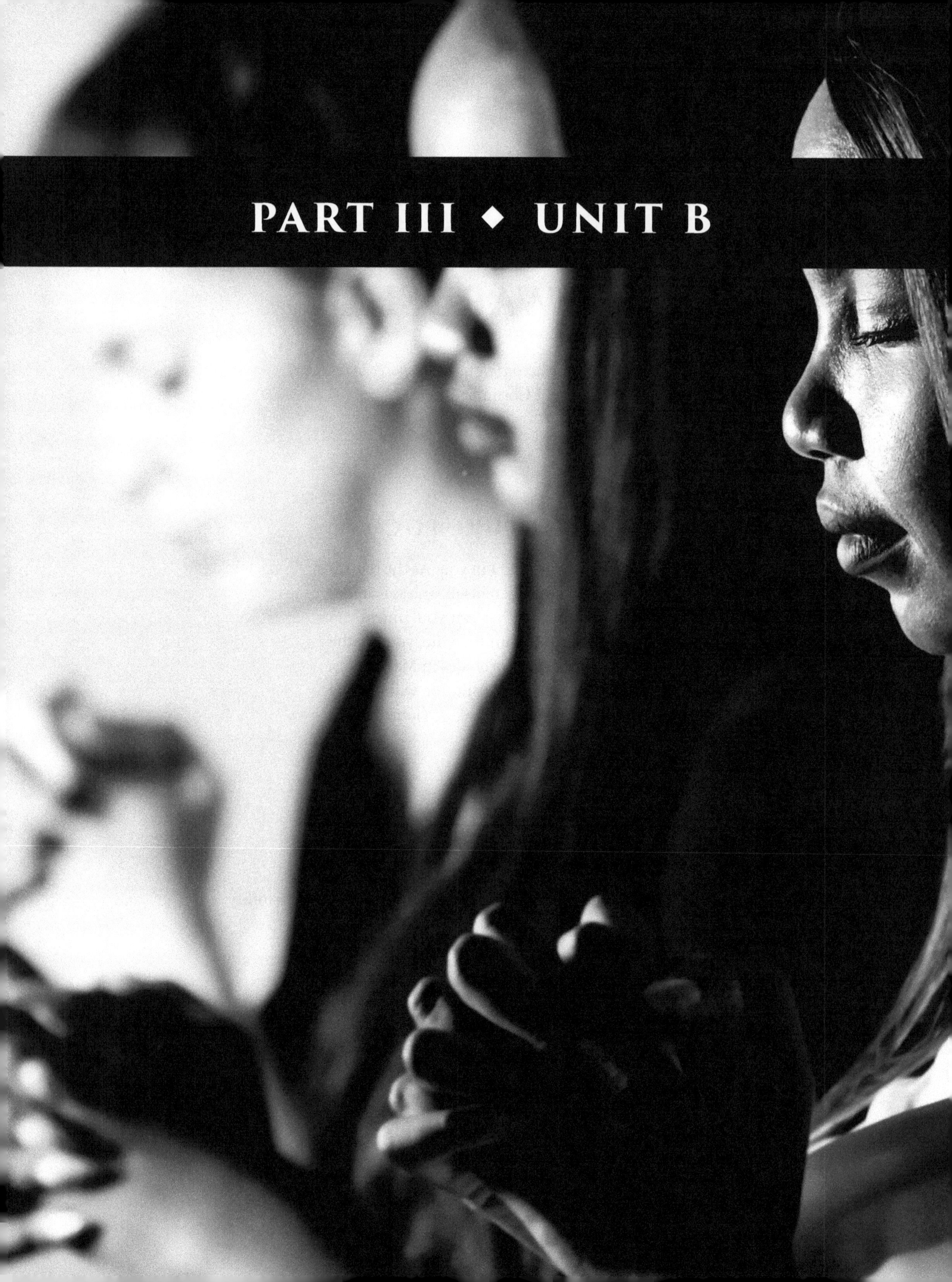

RELATIONSHIP WITH GOD

INTRODUCTION

Ultimately, Christian discipleship is a personal decision to follow Christ. It requires a commitment to continue following Him faithfully by one's own endeavor. 3,000 may have joined the church collectively in total on the day of Pentecost, but each one of those converts had to devote him/herself to the process of discipleship on his/her own. It is the responsibility of each disciple to take up his/her cross daily and follow the Lord (Matthew 10:38; 16:24; Luke 14:27).

As discussed in other units of study, each person has to receive and believe the gospel message individually, and each must confess Christ as Lord for him/herself. Each must also recognize him/herself as a part of the body of Christ and exercise the unique gift(s) bestowed by the Holy Spirit as a vital part of that body. Most importantly, each believer is responsible for maintaining his/her growth and maturation in pursuit of Christ. Accordingly, it is essential for all disciples to practice spiritual disciplines to grow in the faith. Naturally, as a daily regimen has to be maintained for a child to grow healthy and strong, so too must a spiritual newborn in Christ maintain a daily, spiritual regimen. Below are tried and tested principles to live by that will promote and sustain good Christian living. Let us study them:

1. PRINCIPLES TO LIVE BY – A DAILY SPIRITUAL REGIMEN

A. Quiet Time with God

A key component of personal discipleship is that of establishing a quiet time with the heavenly Father. In other words, each believer needs to set aside a time of prayer, meditation, Bible study, and solitude in the presence of the Lord, one-on-one. Setting up a time to meet God may sound strange. After all, He is not an ordinary person we can contact and put on our calendar. He is the Lord God Most High. Nevertheless, while the Lord God is transcendent (above all, overall), He is also the imminent Holy Spirit. He is present everywhere (Psalm 139:1-7). Jesus taught us to pray to Him as our Father. Therefore, if we set aside time for ourselves to pray to and commune with Him, we will find that He will commune with us (John 14:23; Acts 17:27; Jeremiah 29:13; Revelation 3:20). The preparation is on our part, not the Lord's, so we need to pay attention to meeting Him.

Here are simple but effective ways to meet with the Lord in quiet time:

- Find a quiet place with minimum disturbance to meet with the Father.

A meeting place with God does not have to be exotic or elaborate in terms of décor. The more natural and simple it is, the better. It helps you focus more on why you are there, rather than what needs to be there in terms of furnishings etc. Some dedicate a room they set up as a prayer room and only use it as such. However, a particular area of a room, a chair in a corner, an attic, a basement, patio, a park bench, an empty church sanctuary during the day or the bathroom are all areas some have reserved for quiet times. The key is to find a quiet place away from everyone and anything else that would interrupt you during your quiet time with the Father. Minimize disturbances:

- o   Turn on voicemail on phones/cell phones or turn them off
- o   Turn off televisions, radios, DVDs, electronic games etc.
- o   Tell family and friends not to disturb you except for an emergency during that time
- o   Have your Bible, notebook, journal, pen or tablet with you

- Decide on a time when you will meet consistently

While you may meet with the Father anytime and anywhere, it is good to have a set time to meet Him for your time alone. When it is left to chance, too many competing activities crowd our time with the Lord. Many have found the early morning hours to be ideal. The advantages of the early morning meeting are:

- o   The significance of rising early to meet the Lord in prayer
- o   Starting the day with the Lord first
- o   The quietness of the morning
- o   The precedent set in Scripture (Genesis 19:2, 27; Exodus 24:4; Psalm 57:8; 63:1; Isaiah 26:9; Jeremiah 7:13; John 8:2)
- o   Before the business of the day sets in
- o   To gain spiritual direction and guidance for each day

Similar benefits may be experienced at other times of the day/night. Some stay-at-home parents find that their best quiet times are when everyone in the household has left for work/school. The house is quiet, and they are alone after the morning rush. Others are more nocturnal and find the late hours of the night better times to reflect on the day past and to prepare for the day ahead. Whichever time is more suitable ought to be decided and used.

✎   Begin with a short simple prayer of adoration and thanksgiving

Begin by thanking the Lord for the gift of a new day of life and for His protection and preservation through the past night. Try not to slip into a "laundry list" of needs prayer unless you are so burdened or led of the Spirit to intercede on some matter. Scriptures such as Lamentations 3:23; Psalm 57:7, 8; 63:1-3, and John 8:2 can be drawn on to focus the mind on meeting God in the morning and adoring Him for the privilege of being able to do so. The fact that He saved us through His Son and desires a relationship with us is more than enough reason to give praises to God on rising. Here are some examples:

> Open thou my eyes that I may behold the wondrous things written out of thy law. (Psalm 119:18)

> Search me oh God and know my heart; try me and know my thoughts and lead me in the way everlasting. (Psalm 139:23)

> Thy word is a lamp to my feet and a light to my path. (Psalm 119:105)

> Blessed art Thou, oh Lord teach me thy statutes. (Psalm 119:12)

The Psalms, especially 119 are replete with excellent introductory prayers you may use to commence your quiet time.

✎   Study the Gospel of St. John

Especially for new believers, John's Gospel proves to be an excellent exposé on the life of Jesus Christ. John, the writer, is very clear that he wrote the account of Jesus' life so those who read it may believe that:

> Jesus is the Christ, the Son of God, and that believing you may have life in His name. (John 20:31)

In the Gospel of John, we meet the divine Jesus, the Word (Greek = logos), that is, the One who is the consummate wisdom and power in union with God, the minister of all creation, the ruler of the universe and the cause of all that exist in the world both physical and ethical. In Greek thought, John presents Jesus as the total explanation of all that may be understood of God, mankind, and all creation. He is the reason and cause of all things. He is the Word made flesh that dwells among us whose glory is of God, the Father, full of grace and truth (John 1:1-3, 14, 18).

Then too in the Gospel narrative, John portrays a very human Jesus engaging the ordinary and the outcast, the noble and the notable. He does so with deep compassion and compelling concern. Nowhere else in the other gospel accounts can we read Jesus' one-one-one dialogues with people, and His self-declarations that give deep insight into His self-concept as in John's account. John gives us an intimate portrait of our Lord from the one who was called the beloved disciple and who reclined on His bosom in devotion.

Since a disciple is a follower of Jesus, then a close-up view of the Lord as presented in John is best (John 21:20; 13:22). Read the book of John in small portions. Studying an entire chapter at a time may be unnecessary. The point here is to study Jesus, not complete the readings about Him. It may be best to study small units of scripture at a time indicated by where the natural breaks in the narrative are.

✎   Be conscious of the Holy Spirit as you read and study

Recall from the study on the Holy Spirit that He is the One who convicts and convinces us of the truth of the Word of God. He also draws us to the Father. His work of regeneration also involves the renewing of the mind by helping us to understand spiritual truths, which cannot be discerned by mere human intellect (1 Corinthians 2:14-16). God has concealed some deep truths regarding Himself and His work of salvation in His Word.

It takes the spiritual illuminating power of the Holy Spirit to open our eyes to those mysteries much the same way Jesus did when He taught His disciples (Luke 8:9-10; Matthew 13:51, 52; Luke 10:21-24). In the same way, Jesus has sent the Holy Spirit to enable our understanding (John 15:26-27).

Therefore, be aware of His indwelling presence and cultivate your spiritual ears to listen to His gentle unveiling of truth in your heart. He will lead you into all truth, which convicts the world of sin, righteousness, and judgment to come.

✎   Journalize thoughts, insights, questions, doubts encountered

As you read the book of John, allow the scriptures to engage your intellect reflecting deeply on what is read. Write down any truths learned and any thoughts that emerge freely. Jot down questions or concerns for further study or research. Note any scriptures that stand out and commit these to memory. Apply any principles learned in your daily living. For example, the story of the blind man in Chapter 9 may provoke these questions:

o   Am I blind?

o   Am I unwilling to see the truth that the Lord presents plainly before me?

o   What resistance do I show to deny Christ in my life or the lives of others?

o   Am I ashamed to testify about the Lord?

o   Do I judge people's misfortunes by appearances and according to cultural norms or according to the Word of God?

o   Why did the disciples think the man had sinned and, therefore, was responsible for his blindness from birth?

Journalizing enables one to map growth and development. Documenting one's insights and experiences is compiling literary photographs, which may be reflected on at later times. By so doing, the journal will show growth in understanding over time as questions are answered. It will mark the points in life where faith may have deepened, when difficulties were weathered, and how triumphs were achieved.

Journalizing will etch footprints that may be retraced over a period of time with good benefit. Often, insights that were written at one time will reveal their profound nature at another. You will be amazed at the very rich thoughts you had as your mind was illumined by the Holy Spirit in your times of study and meditation.

At other times of reflection, you will marvel at how naïve you may have been and how many of the questions that stumped you initially can now be well answered. For example, the Gospels to a limited extent document the growth in the lives of the apostles of Jesus as they developed from mere fishermen primarily, to bold, competent witnesses able to articulate the scriptures to the amazement of the Sanhedrin (Act 4:13). A personal journal can serve a similar purpose.

✎   Pray about what you've read about

Having written down thoughts, questions, and insights, spend time praying about what was read and studied. It is quite easy to offload our laundry list of requests to the Lord telling Him everything we want, wish, and desire. However, we need to cultivate a more disciplined way to communicate with God first. Since we are His disciples, His will ought to be our highest priority. His Word, the Bible, reveals His will to and for us. It contains God's burden for His people and His desire for those who are yet to become His people.

Thus, when we read His Word, we want to be careful to see whether what we have read communicates His will for our present circumstances. For example, if we go back to John 9, our prayer could be asking the Lord to open our eyes so that we are not blind to what He wants us to see. It may be to give us the boldness to be unashamed that we were blind but now we have met Jesus, our spiritual eyes have been opened. It may be to pray for parents bound by societal pressure or for religious leaders unwilling to accept that God works in unusual ways, which challenge our traditions and beliefs. Praying this way focuses our attention on the issues that matter to the Lord. It redirects us from our selfish desires to the matters of the kingdom that are concerned with the life and death of the people of the world including those closest to us. Thus, the more minute issues of our lives are brought into perspective. The scriptures warn us against vain prayers that are so selfishly motivated that God does not answer them (James 4:3). Once we have ministered to the Lord, we are free to express all our cares to Him. He is interested in all our concerns. We are admonished:

> Casting all your care upon Him, for He cares for you. (1 Peter 5:7)

> For we do not have not a High Priest who cannot sympathize with our weaknesses, but was in all points tempted as we are, yet without sin. Let us therefore come boldly to the throne of grace, that we may obtain mercy and find grace to help in time of need. (Hebrews 4:15-16)

We are further assured that the Father knows what we need before we ask; therefore, we need not worry (Matthew 6:8, 25-34). Further, the Holy Spirit Himself intercedes on our behalf with groanings that are too deep for words, so that the will of the Father is realized in our lives (Romans 8:26-27). He works all things together for our good because we love Him, and He loves us.

Hence, in this relationship, we need not panic that our cares will be unaddressed. Rather, we only need to trust and direct our prayers on the behalf of the needs of the kingdom so that His will may be done on earth as it is in heaven (Matthew 6:9-13). It is amazing how when we discipline ourselves to pray according to the will of God as expressed in His Word that it shapes our prayers and the focus of our lives. We become better witnesses for the kingdom of God when we pray as directed by the Word of God, and we read daily in a consistent, systematic way.

Listen to God's Voice

Spending quiet time with the Lord is also about listening in silence. After you pray out loud, spend some time quietly listening to the Spirit of the Lord speaking to you. As was stated earlier, you need to be aware that God talks to us through His Holy Spirit who is our counselor and guide. By listening in anticipation, we cultivate an ear to hear the Lord speak to us. Don't be perturbed by the sound of the noises around you that fill those moments. In time, they will become background noises. Don't be distracted by your own thoughts. In time, they too will become instruments of God's communication to you. Often, in such moments, the Lord may impress others on your heart/mind whom you may need to speak to. You will need to share what He has told you with them.

B. Tell Someone What The Lord Has Done For You

As we grow in grace and in the knowledge of our Lord and Savior Jesus Christ, it is important that we share our faith with others in a natural and forthright manner. As an outgrowth of your time with the Lord, you will find a growing desire to invite others to experience that same joy that you find in the presence of the Lord. You need not think you have to become an evangelist or a Bible scholar to share your Christian faith.

On the contrary, you only need to tell others what happened to you since you became a disciple of Jesus Christ. A genuine Christian experience is impactful and meaningful to others. It is often far more effective than a theological discourse of the Bible. These are expressions of objective truth, but your personal testimony is a subjective, personal experience of that truth in your life that cannot be refuted. Consider the impact of the Samaritan woman who ran throughout the town inviting people to, "Come see a man who told me everything I did. Is not this the Christ?" (John 4.29). Think about the blind man who told people what Jesus did to open his eyes (John 9:11, 15, 17, 30-33).

In each case, simply relating the story of what the Lord had done was enough to change entire towns and bring them to Jesus. You can do the same; your story is valuable and vital. Tell it!

STUDENT ACTIVITIES
—PERSONAL REFLECTION—

The entire body of Christ increases and is edified as each individual part functions and supplies its yield to the corporate body of the church. The effectual working of the Holy Spirit in each disciple causes the entire body to grow up in love complimenting its head even Christ. Your personal growth or lack of growth determines the health of the entire Christian body. Think about how your individual actions affect the assembly where you worship.

MEMORY GEM

As newborn babes, desire the pure milk of the word, that you may grow thereby, if indeed you have tasted that the Lord is gracious.
(1 Peter 2:2-3)

JOURNALIZE YOUR JOURNEY

Write down the meaningful insights you gained and what has impacted you most in this study segment.

Blessed is the man who…in His law he meditates day and night. (Psalm 1:1-2)

FURTHER STUDY (OPTIONAL)

✎ Read the story of Chuck Colson in his book *Born Again*

✎ Read *Betrayed*, Stan Telchin, Tuscan, 2007

✎ Consider writing your story of conversion. It may become a powerful testimony of the grace of God that encourages others to believe as well.

PART III

THE CALL TO STEWARDSHIP

*Separate to Me Barnabas and Saul for the work
to which I have called them. (Acts 13:2)*

SCRIPTURE FOCUS

As they ministered unto the Lord and
fasted, the Holy Spirit said, "Now
separate to Me Barnabas and Saul for
the work to which I have called them."
Then, having fasted and prayed, and
laid hands on them, they sent them
away.   (Acts 13:2, 3)

PROMPTER GUIDE

In this unit of study, you will learn about personal
responsibility in the local church regarding

1. **PERSONAL EVANGELISM**
2. **CORPORATE EVANGELISM**
3. **MISSIONS**

PART III ◆ UNIT C

SALT AND LIGHT

RELATIONSHIP WITH THE WORLD

INTRODUCTION

By now, it should be evident that discipleship is a dynamic, ongoing activity in the life of the believer in Jesus Christ. It does not end once a believer has been schooled in the doctrines of the faith and has begun to observe them in his/her individual life. Rather, it continues in such a way that each discipled believer, in turn, disciples others they encounter in the course of daily living. This activity is called evangelizing – the act of sharing the good news of the gospel with the world. This is a simple definition, which may be sufficient for our purposes here. However, Dr. Robert Fern offers a more comprehensive definition from Canon Bryan Green in his book, *The Power of Cooperative Evangelism* (EMIS):

> *Evangelism is the proclaiming of Christ Jesus in the power of the Holy Spirit that men should come to put their trust in God through him, accepting him as Savior and him as Lord of personal life and in the corporate fellowship of the church.*[iii]

Let us study this activity so that we may practice it as we are expected to do as disciples of Jesus Christ. He commissioned His disciples to do so declaring:

> All authority has been given to Me in heaven and on earth. Go therefore and make disciples of all the nations, baptizing them in the name of the Father and of the Son and of the Holy Spirit, teaching them to observe all things that I have commanded you (Matthew 28:18-20a)

Discipling others with the gospel is neither a mere traditional practice of the church nor is it, as some critics believe, the bigoted attempt to impose our religious beliefs on others. Rather, it is the primary imperative of the Lord Jesus Christ Himself.

It is His divine will that the gospel of the kingdom is proclaimed to every living creature of every ethnic group throughout the world. The growth of the kingdom is dependent on it, and the appearance of the kingdom in visible fullness awaits it. It is not the will of the Father that any should perish but that all should come to repentance (2 Peter 3:9; Matthew 24:14).

---

iii   Bryan Green, The Power of Cooperative Evangelism, (EMIS)

Notice that Jesus' emphasis in His commission stated above is threefold: making disciples, baptizing those disciples, and teaching those disciples to observe all that He commanded. Therefore, evangelizing is the Christian disciple's principal responsibility. It is the proclamation of the gospel so that disciples are made, baptized, and taught to observe the Word, the will, and the way of Christ.

Every Christian was evangelized with the gospel. Hence, every Christian must evangelize others as the Spirit leads, exercising the very gifts the Spirit has endowed every believer for that very purpose. It may be done individually, (personal evangelism) collectively (corporate evangelism) via formal missionary efforts locally and abroad (missions), and it must consist of both the proclamation and the practice of what is believed and preached. Each of these methods of evangelism is briefly reviewed here in this study. However, the understanding and mastery of each will require specialized study and practice.

In all of them, the goal is two-fold:

a. To commend the saving love of God in Christ Jesus to all that will receive it (Romans 5:8)

b. To warn of the condemnation of those who refuse to receive God's Son as Savior (John 3:18-19)

Let us review the methods of evangelism mentioned above.

1. PERSONAL EVANGELISM

✎   One-on-One

The one-on-one interaction of the Christian with his/her unsaved friends, relatives or strangers

a. The personal engagement of a believer with a non-believer(s) sharing the good news of the kingdom of Jesus Christ

b. The act of persuading non-believer(s) to surrender to the Lordship of Jesus as the will of God

c. The believer is moved by the Holy Spirit to share the Word of God informally or formally with others to the saving of their souls

✎   Informal evangelizing

Informal evangelizing takes place in everyday interactions:

a. Telling one's testimony to friends in casual conversations

b. Over a cup of tea/coffee with a neighbor or co-worker

c.   Talking in the bus, train or plane with a fellow traveler

d.   A chance encounter with a perfect stranger

Informal, personal evangelizing occurs wherever and whenever the opportunity arises to share the message of salvation. Each believer must be prepared to be used by the Lord knowing that His plan is the salvation of all.

✎   Formal evangelizing

Formal evangelizing occurs when a mutual appointment is made to discuss the gospel at a neighbor's kitchen table, over a meal, at the office or some other meeting point. Both parties expect to be engaged in discussion about the Bible and what it says regarding one's need for salvation. A small group Bible study may be arranged at work or at a home where the gospel is presented and hopefully accepted.

Whether formal or informal, the "evangelists" need to trust God to orchestrate the interface. Therefore, each believer should always be ready to give everyone an answer concerning the hope of salvation within him/her, in season and out of season (1 Peter 3:15; 2 Timothy 4:2).

Here are some examples in the scriptures of personal, one-on-one encounters:

✎   John 1:40 – Andrew to Simon (brother to brother)

✎   John 1:43 – Phillip to Nathaniel (friend to friend)

✎   John 4:5-42 – Jesus to the woman (stranger to stranger)

✎   John 3:1-21 – Jesus to Nicodemus (Savior to the intellectual/religious)

✎   Acts 8:26-40 – Philip to the Ethiopian eunuch (evangelist to the curious)

✎   Acts 10 – Peter and company to Cornelius' family and friends (evangelist to seeker)

2.   CORPORATE EVANGELISM

Corporate Evangelism is done collectively by the church body. It may happen in several ways and formats:

a.   A series of evangelistic services in which an evangelist is the featured speaker

b.   An organized tract (pamphlet) distribution campaign in a neighborhood

c.   A door to door witnessing campaign where teams of members participate in spreading the gospel during preplanned events

d.   An initiative that comes from the leaders of the church/membership, which mobilizes the corporate body as a result

3. MISSIONS

As the name suggests, missions is another form of evangelism. It refers to the sending of a person or a group of persons to accomplish a specific service(s) (Webster). Evangelism via missions is the sending forth of Christian workers to propagate the gospel, so the people to whom they are sent may be persuaded to receive it and become disciples of Jesus Christ. Throughout the scriptures, there are numerous instances where God sent forth persons to carry His Word to others or to accomplish His will:

- Noah and his family were chosen to save humanity (Genesis 6-8)
- Abraham was to be the father of a new nation (Genesis 12)
- Moses was called to deliver Israel from slavery in Egypt (Exodus 3:9-12)
- Prophets were sent to call nations to repentance (Isaiah 6:9; Jeremiah 1)
- Priests and kings were anointed to lead God's people (Exodus 28; 2 Samuel 2)
- Jesus the Son of God was God's greatest envoy (Hebrews 3:1-2)
- Apostles were sent forth to proclaim the gospel and to establish communities of believers in Jesus' name (Matthew 28:18-20; Luke 24:44-48; Mark 16:15-20; John 20:21)
- Church fathers and mothers have continued the great commission down through the centuries over the past 2000 years to our day.

Currently, even in countries hostile to Christianity, many believers continue to be martyred. Yet, there are those who soldier on at the command of the Captain of our salvation who bids them to do so (Revelation 2:8-13). These ought to be supported and prayed for as they make supreme sacrifices for the kingdom of God and His Christ our Lord.

Then too, there is another form of missions facilitated by advancements in technology. The advent of television, cable networks, the internet, compact audio disc, DVDs, SIM cards, and chips has made it possible to spread the gospel without leaving one's country. More than ever, the church needs to utilize every means of communication and still go to make disciples of all ethnic groups throughout the world.

The advancements in technology have significantly reduced the necessity of having to physically interface with people in foreign lands. However, electronic media can never replace human-to-human contact. Face-to-face communication of the gospel is irreplaceable, especially where there is human need and suffering that Christian love and compassion can address. Many missionaries are also medical personnel, teachers, engineers, builders, activists for justice etc. Others provide and build real life fellowship among believers, which a virtual audience can't give.

STUDENT ACTIVITIES
—PERSONAL REFLECTION—

How can you be an effective witness for Jesus? Wherever you go in life, you can spread, share, and send forth the gospel as an evangelist. Simply being an exemplary example to your household, family members, friends, neighbors, work colleagues, and the world at large is a good place to begin. Who in your social networks know that you are a Christian by what you communicate or spend time viewing? Pray to be used by the Lord as His witness or as an evangelist/missionary. Ensure that all those whom the Lord draw to Him in response to your testimony are discipled and integrated into a sincere local church that is committed to the edifying, equipping, and empowering of believers for their growth and maturation in the Lord Jesus Christ.

MEMORY GEM

You therefore, my son, be strong in the grace that is in Christ Jesus. And the things that you have heard from me among many witnesses, commit these to faithful men who will be able to teach others also.   (2 Timothy 2:1-2)

JOURNALIZE YOUR JOURNEY

Write down the meaningful insights you have gained. What has impacted you most in this study segment?

Blessed is the man who … in His law he meditates day and night. (Psalm 1:1-2)

_____

_____

_____

_____

_____

_____

_____

_____

_____

FOR FURTHER STUDY (OPTIONAL)

Investigate the notable historic missions of the Christian church and seek to discover what made them so, whom God used to affect them, and how. Contemplate how you may be used to impact the world with the gospel as was done by those who have gone before us. Here are some resources to consider reading in your research:

- *The Great Awakenings*, Dr. David Livingston
- *Welch Revival*, George Lisle (Liele), George Muller
- *The Matyr of the Pongas*, Henry Caswell

APPENDIX: EXERCISES

PART I UNIT A – THE GOSPEL MESSAGE

Exercise 1a. (homework)

Read the story of Zacchaeus in Luke 19:1-9.

Answer the following questions and turn in the completed copy to your teacher/class facilitator in the next class.

1. What did Zacchaeus want?
2. What hindered his desire?
3. What actions did he take to overcome his inability?
4. How did Jesus respond to Zacchaeus' efforts?
5. How did Zacchaeus respond to Jesus' request?
6. What do you suppose they discussed over their meal?
7. What was Zacchaeus' fruit of repentance?
8. How did Jesus respond to Zacchaeus' decision (fruit)?

PART I UNIT B – THE GOSPEL OF THE KINGDOM OF GOD

Exercise 1b. (homework)

How far does God want the gospel proclaimed, and how big does He want His kingdom to be?

Read the following scriptures and list the places where the gospel was/is to be proclaimed in your workbooks:

Luke 4:14-21

Luke 4:31-37

Luke 4:44

Luke 8:13

Matthew 4:23-25

Matthew 28:18-20

Acts 1:8

Exercise 1b.2

Complete the scriptures below. Study them to help you understand Satan's diabolical rule in the world and in the lives of those who need to be saved.

1. 2 Corinthians 4:4

Whose minds the god of this age has _____, who do not believe, lest the light of the gospel of the glory of Christ, who is the image of God, should _____ on them.

2. Luke 8:12

Those by the wayside are the ones who _____; then the devil (deceiver) comes and _____ the word out of their _____ lest they should _____.

3. You are of your _____ the _____, and the _____ of your father you want to do. He was a _____ from the beginning, and does not stand in the _____, because there is no _____ in him. When he speaks a _____, he speaks it from his own resources, for he is a _____ and the father of it.

4. 1 Peter 5:8

Be sober, be vigilant; because your _____ the _____ walks about like a _____, seeking whom he may _____.

5. Ephesians 2:1

And you He made alive, who were _____ in _____ and _____, in which you once walked according to the _____ of this world, according to the _____ of the _____ of the air, the _____ who now works in the sons of _____, among whom also we all once conducted ourselves in the [blank] of our flesh, fulfilling the desires of the flesh and of the [blank], and were by nature the children of [blank] just as the [blank].

6. Revelation 12:9

So the [blank] was cast out, that [blank], called the [blank] and [blank], who deceives the whole world; he was [blank] to the earth, and his [blank] were cast out with him.

The above references paint a gloomy picture of the human condition under satanic control. It does not take much imagination to see why the world, in the decadent condition it is in, needs the gospel (Romans 3:10-18). What can you do to help destroy the evil kingdom of Satan? How can you restore the kingdom of God in your life and in the lives of others?

PART I UNIT C – THE GOSPEL OF THE LORD JESUS CHRIST

Exercise 1c. (homework)

Read Acts 7:54, 57-58; 8:1-3; 9:1-31 and answer the following questions about Saul:

1. What was Saul's view of the Jews who worshipped Jesus as Lord?
2. What role did he play in Stephen's martyrdom?
3. What role did he play in the persecution of the church?
4. How did Stephen view Jesus at the time of his death?
5. How is Saul characterized in his opposition to the church?
6. Describe Saul's response to the voice he heard.
7. How did Saul respond verbally to the voice he heard?
8. Who do you suppose he understood the speaker from heaven to be?
9. Describe Saul's change in attitude, vocabulary, and behavior after his Damascus experience.

Exercise 1c.2

Read Matthew 16:13-20 and answer the following questions:

1. What was the prevailing public opinion of Jesus?
2. Who did the disciples think Jesus was?

3. Where did Jesus say Peter's revelation came from?

4. Notice the power and authority that is bestowed on all who acknowledge Jesus Christ for who He truly is.

PART II UNIT A - JOINING THE CHURCH

Exercise 2a. (homework)

Based on the study, answer the following questions:

1. What is doctrine?

2. How important is it to know the doctrine of the apostles?

3. What is the Apostles Creed?

4. What is fellowship?

5. How do you fellowship with the church body?

6. How important is it to eat with other church members?

7. How do simplicity and sincerity play a part in good fellowship?

Exercise 2a.2

Review the story of Ananias and Sapphira (Acts 5:1-11) and answer the following:

1. Compare Barnabas' actions to those of Ananias and Sapphira's. What was similar/different?

2. Why was Peter so draconian with the couple?

3. Why do you suppose they died?

4. What lessons might we learn here?

Exercise 2a.3 (group discussion)

Review the story of Philip in Samaria (Acts 8:1-24) and discuss the following in your group:

1. Who was Simon?

2. What drew him to Philip?

3. Was he truly converted?

4. Was he added to the number?

PART II UNIT D – THE GIFTS OF THE HOLY SPIRIT

Exercise 2d

List the gifts of the Spirit mentioned in the following passages and answer the questions: Romans 12:6-8; 1 Corinthians 12:4-11; Ephesians 4:11; 1 Peter 4:11

1.   Which gifts do you think you have?

2.   According to 1 Corinthians 13, how are the gifts to be exercised?

3.   According to 1 Corinthians 14:1-5, 22-25, which gift should be pursued above all and why?

4.   Why does the apostle Paul describe it as such?

5.   Which gift is recommended to be "coveted"?

6.   Why is the gift of tongues (languages) not better than the gift of prophecy?

7.   What is the primary purpose of the gift of languages? (1 Corinthians 14:22, 4)

8.   Can we pray for specific gifts?

9.   What motivation should drive our requests?

PART III UNIT A – STEWARDSHIP IN THE LOCAL CHURCH

Exercise 3a

Read the story of the talents (Matthew 25:14-30) and answer the following questions:

1.   What was the perception of the businessman who entrusted his servants with his assets?

2.   Why do you suppose that different people got different amounts?

3.   What would the servants who received five and two talents respectively have had to do to double their investments as they did?

4.   What was wrong with the actions of the servant who had received one talent?

5.   How did the master respond to the servants who were industrious as opposed to the one who was indolent?

6.   What is your perception of the servant who buried his talent?

7.   To which servant's attitude are you more closely aligned?

Exercise 3a.2

Review the following text and write down what you think each is saying about the use of time and abilities:

a. Ephesians 5:15, 16

b. 1 Corinthians 10:31

c. Romans 6:13

d. Romans 12:1-11

PART III UNIT B – RELATIONSHIP WITH GOD

Exercise 3b

Review the following text and try to gain a sense of the writers' devotional experiences in each case.

Genesis 24:62, 63

Joshua 1:1-8

Psalm 1

Psalm 63:1-6

Psalm 77:12

Psalm 119:23, 48, 78

Psalm 143:5

1 Timothy 4:1-15

Exercise 3c

The class may be divided into groups to study each scenario above and make observations afterward. A spokesperson from each group may report on their findings to the class.

Review Questions: (Study each encounter)

1. What made each encounter personal?
2. What prompted the conversations?
3. Was any pressure applied to the persons involved?
4. In which cases were the initiatives human and in which were they divine?
5. How were the "evangelists" received by those who shared the good news with them?
6. Which was formal?
7. Which was informal?

Exercise 3c.2

- Disciples are sent out officially by Jesus (Luke 9:1-6; 10)
- Samaria is evangelized (Acts 8:5-25)
- Outreach Antioch (Acts 11:19-30)

Review Questions

1. Where were the disciples directed to go?

2. Whose idea was it for the disciples to go into the villages?

3. What were they to do specifically?

4. What were they told not to do and why?

5. Who empowered them to preach, heal the sick, and cast out demons?

6. What organization was put in place to manage their efforts?

Exercise 3c.3

How willing are you to serve God in the face of hostility? Here are some examples of missions in the scripture that would inform us to do as the Lord directs through the local and international church bodies to which we belong/serve:

1. Isaiah 6

2. Jeremiah 1:1-10

3. Acts 10 (Peter and company to Cornelius)

4. Acts 8:26-40 (Philip to the Ethiopian eunuch)

5. Acts 11:19-26 (Paul and Barnabas to Antioch)

6. Acts 13:1-5 (Paul and Barnabas to the nations)

7. Acts 13:5-52 (Paul and his team to Asia-Minor)

8. Timothy to various churches (1 Corinthians 4:17; 2 Corinthians 1:1; Philippians 2:19-20)

9. Titus to Corinth (2 Corinthians 8:16-24)

It would also be helpful to study historic missions that were undertaken by outstanding men and women of God who carried the gospel to nations abroad.

NEW MEMBERS ORIENTATION

This activity is designed to give you a proper introduction to your new life and church fellowship. Now that you are a disciple of Jesus, you have to live a disciplined life as a member of a local church, which is part of the universal body of Christ made up of believers everywhere. Therefore, you will need to appreciate that as a member of such a church, you have an important role to play or functions to perform in your church. However, you will need training to better understand and fulfill the responsibilities you now have or will shortly be given.

This is precisely what this entire program of discipleship training is about. Specifically, this introductory segment is designed to orient you properly to the ethos of your local church assembly and the study material. This segment provides you with answers to any questions you may have at the onset. Therefore, you should not by-pass these orientation lessons.

Orientation sets the tone for the remainder of your studies. It is vital for your beginning or first steps on this discipleship journey. This will become more evident when you are mature enough to lead others along the same path you are now being led.

Humility is the key to learning. Inquire intently but learn humbly as the example of Jesus shows. He always referred all things to the Father, whose will He came to earth to follow in every step He took on His earthly journey (Philippians 2:5-11; John 4:34; Luke 22:42).

Be punctual and patient. Sometimes, aspects of the material might have to be repeated to ensure you thoroughly grasp them. Other times, you may get the correct understanding the first time it is explained. However, discipleship classes offer a group learning experience; it is a process of learning together. Those who are quick students might have to wait on those who are not as quick.

Do not be afraid to pose questions. Go ahead even if you risk appearing silly. Sometimes, an assumed silly question can help another student immensely – even the teacher!

Orientation Obligations

1. Sign-in on the attendance sheet
2. Complete/turn in the membership data form
3. Receive a schedule of discipleship classes
4. Receive Unit l A worksheet and the ABC's of Salvation (complete and return)
5. Receive any general information

BIBLIOGRAPHY

i. Harris, R. L., Harris, R. L., Archer, G. L., & Waltke, B. K., *Theological Wordbook of the Old Testament* (electronic ed.) (490). Chicago: Moody Press, 1999, c1980.

ii. Vine, W.E., *Vine's Complete Expository Dictionary of Old and New Testament Words*, Thomas Nelson Publishers, 1996 (pg. 525)

iii. Ferm, Robert O., *The Power of Cooperative Evangelism*, EMIS, 2002